Making Sense

of

Unseen Poems

by

Rex W Last

Reviews of volume one – *Making Sense of Poetry*

'A "must have" book which encourages the reader to explore poetry in greater depth. To pursue its meaning and thence to delight rather than bewilder.

'Rex Last has written with humour and alacrity. I shall now unearth my poetry books long since assigned to dusty shelves.'
(Margaret Holman, Amazon review)

'I liked that the author, understanding how boring poetry could be at times, adds humour to his explanations at regular intervals. This is an effective way of teaching, as it made me appreciate what he tried to explain faster. It also made me feel refreshed while I read, as I had some good laughs. Furthermore, I liked that the author included exercises on the interpretation of poems and their solutions to enable readers to test themselves, having gained the knowledge that the book sought to teach.

'There was nothing to dislike about this book, and I enjoyed it thoroughly. The author structured his message very well and executed it with perfection. ... I recommend this book for people who are interested in Poetry.'
(Reviewer, onlinebookclub.org)

'*Making Sense of Poetry* is full of down-to earth wisdom. It brooks no nonsense. Its examples are perfectly chosen. The authorial voice is friendly but authoritative. The structure, with its insightful interludes, is just right. A fine educational primer.'
(Robert Saxton, poet)

About the Author

Rex W Last was Professor of Modern Languages in the University of Dundee from 1981-1991 after nearly two decades in the German Department of Hull University. He has written books on topics from Hans Arp, Dadaism, Erich Maria Remarque and Erich Kästner to artificial intelligence and computer-assisted instruction for the language teacher. He was also the editorial director of a London publishing company specialising in German literature and culture.

He edited the pioneering computerised *Arthurian Bibliography* and has translated a number of books including Willy Brandt's wartime memoirs, a study of Max Ernst, a biography of the early peace campaigner Bertha von Suttner, and an account of West German President Gustav Heinemann.

Now retired as Professor Emeritus, he writes computer programs, wartime adventure novels set in Germany, designs websites and has written countless articles for a number of computer magazines. For most of its existence, he was editor of *PCW User*, the official magazine of the late lamented Amstrad PCW computer.

Visit his web pages at www.locheesoft.com.

Table of Contents

Acknowledgements

I am most grateful to Robert Saxton for permission to quote in full his sonnet 'Early Riser'. An approachable poet who wears his gift lightly, he has published a number of collections of poems which can be obtained from Amazon or the Poetry Book Society.

As ever, I should like to thank my beta test readers: Oksana Last (for subediting, too), Margaret and Derick Holman and Liz Gordon.

You will find after most chapters an interlude on a specific topic, which offers you the chance to test your knowledge. Answers to questions are to be found in the appendices.

This book is accompanied by a series of YouTube videos which act as a companion to the two *Making Sense of Poetry* guides. They are available on Youtube. Search for Rex Last study guides.

More information about the author and his recent publications will be found at the end of this book and on his website at www.locheesoft.com.

Introduction

In the first guide of this series, *Making Sense of Poetry*, I set out a series of simple techniques which demonstrated how to interpret poetry at a basic level, and this guide continues that process from a different angle. In this second book, I shall be showing you how to use the knowledge you all have tucked away in a corner of your brains which will sharpen your insights into poetry, and I shall also be challenging you to read poetry as widely as possible, because that is the very best way of enhancing your skills and (let's be practical) improving your chances of getting half decent marks in course work and examinations on this tricky subject of unseen poems.

Let me recap in some detail the approach to poetry which I recommended you should apply. Remember that this is not a list of tests to be enforced for each and every poem – not all of the tests work all the time, as poetry is not like a scientific formula. You have to become flexible in your use of these aids to interpretation as different poems, and most often the poem itself will tell you which items on my list apply most usefully in each case.

'Unseen poems', the title of this study guide, does not signify hidden gems, in other words poems that have undeservedly (or otherwise) not seen the light of day for many years. It refers, of course, to one of the exercises taught at school and college level in which you are thrown to the wolves, so to speak, by being given a poem or two to interpret which you have not seen before. My objective here is to make that exercise much more of a pleasure for you than a chore and to give you the tools to improve your insights into all poetry, seen or unseen.

Below you'll find the list of aspects of a poem you should investigate, which form the 'twelve commandments'. Each is optional, and depends on the poem you are studying. Flexibility is the name of the game, and if you can acquire the skill to learn which of the options below to adopt for a particular poem, you are well on the way to a useful interpretation.

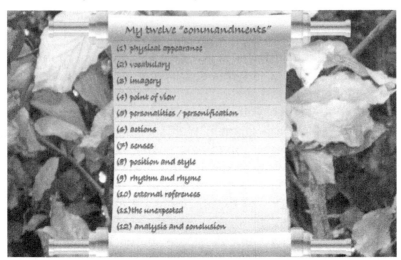

My twelve "commandments"

(1) physical appearance

(2) vocabulary

(3) imagery

(4) point of view

(5) personalities / personification

(6) actions

(7) senses

(8) position and style

(9) rhythm and rhyme

(10) external references

(11) the unexpected

(12) analysis and conclusion

Physical appearance

First, examine the poem as a shape on the page and see if that offers you any clues to its meaning and purpose. For example, as we shall see in our first examples, if the poem is fourteen lines long, that in itself throws up clues to its interpretation. More of that in a moment or two. Next, examine the punctuation: for example, is there a succession of easy-flowing end-stop lines, or are there staccato sequences of questions and exclamations? ('End-stop lines' contain a unit of meaning within the individual line, rather than running on from one line to another, for which the technical term is 'enjambement'.)

Also, when considering the punctuation, also check on which words in the poem are capitalised, and why. Much more about that later.

Title

If the poet is considerate enough to give the poem a title, that is the obvious place to start putting together a provisional idea of what the content might be about. Don't assume that the title can do more than that, for quite often it's just a starting point.

For example, Wordsworth's poem in six stanzas, 'The Lesser Celandine', is not just about a pretty yellow flower, it ranges far and wide, generalising about the significance of the way it emerges and blooms on a much bigger canvas. And if a title is lacking, try examining the first couple of lines of the poem to get a general idea of what it is about, or at least, what its departure point is.

Vocabulary

This is a substantial topic, and my suggestion for the best way into the poem's vocabulary is to consider applying the concept of word fields. In the illustration from YouTube below, you will see a typical example of a word field, with a general term at the top of the expanding list, followed by three sample sub-fields, and seven sample sub-fields of the head.

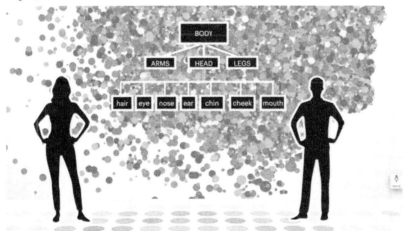

Again, this is poetry, not science, so you may well find that it is trickier to winkle out the word fields in a poem than in other aspects of human knowledge. You will find an extended example of how to deal with this issue in Chapter one that follows.

For a fuller discussion of vocabulary, see Chapter seven of the first *Making Sense of Poetry* book and the YouTube poetry introductory videos.

Imagery

Again, we have landed on a big topic and I have tried to simplify it by explaining it in terms of a 'pecking order', or 'dominance hierarchy' to give it its Sunday name. As the phrase suggests, it explains a situation in terms of a kind of class structure, with the most dominant at the top, and so on down the list until you reach the least important and least significant item.

Simile

Starting at the bottom of the pile, so to speak, we deal first with the simile. The whole list of the main categories of image is displayed here, one egg at a time, simile first, then on to metaphor, symbol, allegory and parable, and finally, myth.

The simile states that one thing is 'as, like' another. The two 'things' are separate and the impact is short-lived. They

abound in everyday speech, and most of them have become clichés, when we hardly recognise the origin of the phrase. Common examples are: deaf as a post, run like a rabbit, her eyes shone like diamonds, thick as two short planks, and so the list goes on. Let's examine a famous example from the poetry of

Robert Burns.

'My love is like a red, red rose' his poem begins, and in this case the object of his affections is compared with one aspect of the rose, the fact that it is an ideal of beauty. In this case the simile is not physically like 'my love' at all.

Metaphor

Up next is a metaphor, which asserts that one thing *is* another. 'He is a lion amongst men' is a simple example.

One of the more complex examples in literature is the speech of the arch cynic Jaques in *As You Like It*. His metaphor for the world and human life is that of the stage, and he asserts that 'All the world's a stage, And all the men and women merely players.'

These actors on the stage begin as a babbling baby and end as a gibbering senile old man. This he perceives as an endlessly repeating cycle. It's not the sunniest view of humanity I have come, across but it is a compelling extended set of metaphors none the less.

The characters on the stage which represents the world begin as babes in arms.

Allegory and parable

Then come allegory and parable, in which the entire story has a parallel meaning.

Christian's journey through manifold challenges and difficulties in *The Pilgrim's Progress*, by John Bunyan, published in 1678, is an allegory of a good man's challenging pathway through life towards 'the Celestial city' of the life ever after.

And, in the New Testament of the Bible, the parables are simple tales with a general meaning which act as a way of teaching the messages of the Gospel.

The Good Samaritan, for example, tells of a man set upon by robbers and left to perish by the roadside. Many travellers walk past on the other side of the road, but a member of the much maligned Samaritans stops and ministers to the victim. The message of the tale is to pose the question: Who is my real neighbour?

Symbol

And then comes the symbol, which extends way beyond the individual work. The red rose symbolises beauty and that too figures in individual works but it also exists independently as an ideal, which has a life outside the individual work and can be poached by any writer for demonstrating those qualities which it embodies.

Myth

Top of the pecking order of imagery is the 'myth', which offers an entire picture of where we came from, how it happened, and where we might be aiming for in the future. The Christian world view is one such myth (without implying it is either true or false), as were those of the Gods of ancient Greeks and Romans.

As I hope you can see from the screenshot, the simile has an immediate but passing significance, the metaphor equates the subject and its metaphorical parallel. The balance of power, so to speak, shifts with the symbol which, as I have just indicated, can reach way beyond the individual work. Finally comes the myth which exists outside the individual work altogether.

Point of view – First person

Is the poem written in the first, second or third person (I, you, he/she/it)? Quite often, poems of the nineteenth century and before address a particular person or object as a way of highlighting its significance. First person first, here as a witness only. In these illustrations, you will find that I have tweaked the notion of the world of the poem as a stage on which the action (or lack of it) takes place.

In the illustration, you can see a representation of a first person narrator as a witness. The poem being used by way of illustration is the folk song lament of a young maiden for a false lover:

> Early one morning
> just as the sun was rising,
> I heard a young maid sing
> in the valley below.
>
> 'Oh, don't deceive me,
> Oh, never leave me,
> How could you use

A poor maiden so?'

The poet is a detached reporter of what is observed, no more. He doesn't even go across to offer the weeping lass a clean handkerchief.

Next up is the first person as a participant in the work, or as often in fiction, the lead character. The example here is

Wordsworth's poem 'I wandered lonely as a cloud', coming across a carpet of daffodils, delighting in their beauty but also reflecting on his own solitude.

In narrative fiction, the first person view is often employed. A famous, often-quoted example, is *Jane Eyre*, by Charlotte Brontë. The conclusion to the novel begins with the simple statement 'Reader, I married him', that is, Mr Rochester. This approach provides a sense of directness and involvement, but a first person narrator can only tell what he or she can perceive and is not always a reliable narrator.

Point of view – second person

Often in lyric poetry, the lover is addressed directly by the narrator in the poem. By the way, the narrator is quite separate from the poet, the person who writes the poem. You will find a famous example of this in Chapter one of this guide.

Point of view – third person

This next still from one of the YouTube presentations depicts an example of the third person as a witness, who describes from a detached viewpoint what is going on. In this particular case, Tennyson's famous 'Charge of the Light Brigade', it would not be advisable for our narrator to get too close to the action at all.

There are several variations on third person narration, but most of them are to be found in narrative fiction, and are beyond the scope of this guide. For a basic introduction, see the topic 'Narration' on Wikipedia.

Personalities and personification

How many 'characters' are there in the poem? Very often, as in the case of Shakespearean sonnets, there are two of them: the narrator (often in the first person) and his lover. Mostly there is just the poet or an invisible narrator. In poetry, the characters tend to be very sketchily defined, and sometimes not described at all.

Actions

What actually takes place in the poem? Unlike drama and fiction which are preoccupied with 'what happens next', a lot of lyric poetry is contemplative and not about a specific sequence of events culminating in a climatic point at the end.

Senses

Which of the five senses occur in the poem? They are sight, hearing, smell, touch, taste. I also speculate that there is a 'sixth sense' (I am not referring to the clever film of that title here), in other words looking into the mind and thoughts of a character or a sequence of ideas, rather than outward into the world.

Position and style

This item is not so much about what is significant in a poem, it is more concerned with where that significance occurs. That's a bit of a mouthful, and the best way of making some sense of this is to keep an eye open for the example from Milton's *Paradise Lost* near the beginning of Chapter three, or the closing passage of Chapter eight's poem 'The Deserted Village'.

Rhythm and rhyme

You may be a little surprised to see these two related items so far down the list of significances, but I take the view that the technical aspects of the stress patterns in poetry are not something that you need to explore in depth. Some basic knowledge, though, is a good thing. Let us begin with the patterns of English speech and how well they can be made to fit into a poetic convention.

Starting with Shakespeare, a lot of his work is in poetic form, and it coincides well with the way in which English functions by employing alternating unstressed and stressed syllables. Here are the first couple of lines from a sonnet we shall be examining in detail in Chapter one:

Shall I compare thee to a summer's day?
Thou art more lovely and more temperate:
Rough winds do shake the darling buds of May,
And summer's lease hath all too short a date:

If you read those lines to yourself slowly, you'll see a clear pattern emerging. If I use the convention of marking a stressed syllable with a '/' sign and an unstressed one with an 'x', this is what happens:

x / x / x / x / x /

An iambic pentameter has five 'feet', the basic unit of a line, each of which has an unstressed syllable followed by a stressed syllable. Fair enough, but you don't have to wade through all the technical variations on this model used by different poets, just note it and how it can vary.

Then there is the rather embarrassing case of *Hiawatha,* an epic poem by Henry Longfellow which annoyingly uses exactly the opposite pattern, the trochee. This little fellow has two beats per foot, but they are the opposite way round to the iamb, with the result that it sounds something like this:

Slowly o'er the simmering landscape
Fell the evening's dusk and coolness,
And the long and level sunbeams
Shot their spears into the forest,
Breaking through its shields of shadow
Rush into each secret ambush,
Searched each thicket, dingle, hollow;
Still the guests of Hiawatha
Slumbered in the silent wigwam.

Read it aloud, and the effect is at first novel and interesting, but after a time it becomes contrived and annoying. Padding words are frequently inserted (the 'and' in line three is just one example), and there is a feeling that the poem proceeds relentlessly on without any pause for breath or variation in tone.

The trochee used here stands the iamb on its head, and it works like this, a stressed syllable followed by an unstressed syllable:

$$/ \ \ x \ \ / \ \ x \ \ / \ \ x \ \ / \ \ x$$

There are four feet to the line in *Hiawatha*, making it a trochaic tetrameter (tetra = four).

You do have to be aware of rhythmic patterns, but I do not suggest you get lost in the esoteric fog of variations to the iambic pentameter or whatever, since oddities of rhythm – even verse which seems to follow no rules – can readily be spotted, especially when the poet is seeking to create a special effect.

External references

The Bible, Classical Greek and Roman cultures, Ancient Egypt, old systems of measurement, changes in word meaning, and much more appear under this heading. These topics are explored further in Interludes three and four.

The unexpected

Here's a simple example. What is a 'dashboard'? Of course, in a car it's the panel containing the dials and so forth in what petrol heads are pleased to call the cockpit. But if you consider the word for a moment, the prefix 'dash' seems a little odd.

Go back to the nineteenth century, and if you saw the word used in a poem, you might scratch your head again with puzzlement. It originates in the wooden or leather board set across the front of a horse-drawn carriage to prevent mud and water being dashed against the driver and passengers.

Or, how do you react when the manger in which Christ was born is described as 'rude'? What are those sheep in the corner up to? Words change their meaning over time, and in this case 'rude' = 'rough', 'simple'. and of course academics have a mouthful of a phrase for it: 'semantic shift'.

You may already have come across this meaning of rude in the carol 'As with Gladness Men of Old', which refers to the baby Jesus' bed as 'a manger rude and bare', to the delight of small choirboys. You will be able gradually to demystify a whole range of archaic vocabulary as you read more and more poems of the past.

The moral of the tale is to proceed with caution when an unexpected word or phrase crops up. Two of the most often quoted examples are 'awful' and 'gay'. In former times, 'awful' meant 'awe-inspiring', and 'gay' had no sexual connotation. It just signified 'cheerful'.

Putting it all together

Then as the final step you have to compose your response to the 'unseen' poem. Those skills are outside the scope of this guide, and I draw your attention to *Making Sense of Essay Writing* in this series, which will help you on your way. For a taste of this guide, go to YouTube and type in the Search box 'Rex Last Essays'.

I do not claim that I have covered every single aspect of poetic interpretation but I do aspire to giving you the main starting points as I see them in arriving at a successful interpretation of a poem, seen or unseen. The rest of this guide focuses on individual poems, interspersed with various tests and trials to improve your poetic analysis skills.

Chapter one – First steps

Let's start with a simple example which I have used in the YouTube series of presentations on the introductory guide, *Making Sense of Poetry*, which can be viewed if you type 'Rex Last study skills' in the YouTube search box.
Here is the text of the poem:

> Shall I compare thee to a summer's day?
> Thou art more lovely and more temperate:
> Rough winds do shake the darling buds of May,
> And summer's lease hath all too short a date
> Sometime too hot the eye of heaven shines,
> And often is his gold complexion dimmed
> And every fair from fair sometime declines,
> By chance, or nature's changing course untrimm'd:
> But thy eternal summer shall not fade,
> Nor lose possession of that fair thou ow'st,
> Nor shall death brag thou wander'st in his shade,
> When in eternal lines to time thou grow'st,
> So long as men can breathe, or eyes can see,
> So long lives this, and this gives life to thee.

If you follow the advice I outlined in the Introduction, you should begin by looking at the poem as a 'slab' of text written in an unknown foreign language, to see if its shape and punctuation alone provides any clues to enable the process of interpretation to get under way.

In this case, the answer is in positive, because if you add up the number of lines, you should come to the total of fourteen. If that means something to you, then you will be more than one step ahead in understanding it, because fourteen lines means that this is a **sonnet,** one of the most popular formats for lyric poetry throughout the history of literature.

Apart from its length, which is ideal for the expression of personal feelings, including love and passion, of course, the sonnet has a particular significance, namely, that it tends to begin by setting out a problem and concludes by offering some kind of solution to it, or at least explaining why any solution is elusive.

If you are familiar with other sonnets by the Bard, you might be aware that the Shakespearean sonnet contains that resolution of the initial question in the last two lines. If you don't, then read this one again, and you will see that the last two lines actually shout out the solution to the reader, particularly as both begin with 'so'. As this paragraph hints, other forms of the sonnet are available, but they do broadly follow the same patterns.

The next step is to examine the poem's title, but if it does not have one, you should check out the opening couple of lines for clues. There is no title to this poem, except for the unhelpful 'Sonnet 14' in a total of 154, so let's examine the first couplet to see what information it offers us on the topic which is to be explored:

> Shall I compare thee to a summer's day?
> Thou art more lovely and more temperate

Before going any further, note that attention to every little detail will help you to increase your understanding of the poem: here the use of 'thee' and 'thou' places it in a past century, but how far back in time it is not at this stage clear. In addition, the language is not dialect, so this tends to rule out a regional poet or one from Scotland or Wales, or elsewhere in the English-speaking world.

This couplet is the first of a series of antitheses (opposites) which run through the poem. A comparison is being made between the poet's lover, who is described as more attractive and more reliable and consistent (temperate) than the summer weather. That is not particularly difficult challenge, given the British weather. As a cynic once said, If you don't like the weather here, wait fifteen minutes.

In this sonnet, the key to an understanding lies with the

vocabulary, and the notion of word fields which I covered in the introduction. Here is a visual representation of the contrasting main word fields the poem contains.

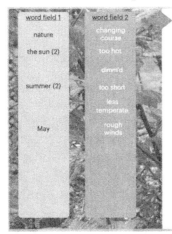

word field 1	word field 2
nature	changing course
the sun (2)	too hot
	dimm'd
summer (2)	too short
	less temperate
May	rough winds

Shall I compare thee to a summer's day?
Thou art more lovely and more temperate:
Rough winds do shake the darling buds of May,
And summer's lease hath all too short a date;
Sometime too hot the eye of heaven shines,
And often is his gold complexion dimm'd;
And every fair from fair sometime declines,
By chance or nature's changing course untrimm'd;
But thy eternal summer shall not fade,
Nor lose possession of that fair thou ow'st;
Nor shall death brag thou wander'st in his shade,
When in eternal lines to time thou grow'st:
   So long as men can breathe or eyes can see,
   So long lives this, and this gives life to thee.

On the left nature heads the word field, and beneath it the sun, and summer and at the bottom of the stack the month of May. The second word field neatly parallels it, providing contrasting phrases which state, for example, that in summer the time is too short and the season less temperate than expected, and so on down the list.

Now I turn to the central part of the poem to explore these antitheses further, and you might notice that this part of the poem can be divided into two: namely, lines 3-8 contain one side of the argument, stating that the summer's day which the poem is about is fickle, unreliable and will one day fade. To quote another of Shakespeare's poems, a song which forms the closing lines of his play *Cymbeline*:

> Golden lads and girls all must,
> As chimney-sweepers come to dust.

We all die in the end, whoever we are, and death is the great leveller. This is one of the enduring themes of poetry, and you may be aware of this famous stanza if you have read Thomas

Gray's 'Elegy in a country Churchyard':

> The boast of heraldry, the pomp of power,
> And all that beauty, all that wealth, e'er gave,
> Awaits alike th' inevitable hour:-
> The paths of glory lead but to the grave.

I have not employed those two quotes just to show off my knowledge, such as it is. I am making two important points. The first is: read poetry widely in order to be better able to set a poem in context, and also in order to heighten your own awareness and sensitivity to poetry generally. See Appendix one for titles of anthologies which will point you in the right direction.

Secondly, display that knowledge by referring to these or other relevant quotes, unless your tutor advises you that the answers for your examination board should focus only on the poem in front of you. At the very least you can state that Shakespeare's theme is one that runs throughout much English lyric poetry, and that the sonnet format is one of the most consistently applied in lyric poetry.

And, as I pointed out in the Introduction, the rhythmic pattern is that of the iambic pentameter and the rhyming pattern is ABAB etc up to line 13, where the last two lines of the poem are AA, they share a rhyme, and this gives added impact to the end of the sonnet.

Now to answer the question I put to you. You should have noticed that the middle section of the poem falls into two parts, the first being six lines long, the second four lines in length. In the first part there is an expansion of line two, namely, that nature is fickle and uncaring, unresponsive to man's feelings.

The second, in which the word 'eternal' is repeated, states a paradox: the lover's beauty and qualities will surely endure eternally, but how is that going to happen? That's the conundrum which the sonnet seeks to resolve in the closing two lines.

In this last couplet, where we are told that praising his lover in verse will give her (or him, it really doesn't matter which) eternal life in this sonnet. Read other sonnets by Shakespeare and see how often he returns to this theme. The word 'this' refers to this poem and the feelings expressed in it. In other words, the sonnet itself is a fitting memorial to his love and he believes it will live on beyond the grave.

Let's move forward a few centuries now to a modern poem which shares at least one feature with our Shakespearean example. But, before that, the first of several interludes which allow you to take a pause for breath and at the same time confront a number of interesting challenges.

Interlude one – Name that poem

Here, is a test of your abilities to determine the origin of not so familiar stanzas (verses) from very well-known poems, drawn from the words to hymns and other sources. Answers are at the back of this guide in Appendix two.

You may spot the source of a quote right away, but don't skip over that question if you do. Take some time to work out how you would have used your detection skills to crack the problem if you hadn't.

Poem one

We begin with a simple demonstration of what I am inviting you to do. There now follows the third verse of a very familiar composition which you all know (I promise):

> Not in this land alone,
> But be God's mercies known,
> From shore to shore!
> Lord make the nations see,
> That men should brothers be,
> And form one family,
> The wide world o'er.

If you do not recognise these rather over-formal words, fear not, you are not alone. Most of the British nation shares your plight. Look first at the number of lines in the stanza: seven. That is an odd number in more ways than one. It is indeed a fairly rare total of lines for a verse, known as a septet. Here is a better clue: one version of the seven-line stanza is called the rhyme royal, and it is curious that this particular example does not fit into that category (hint, hint) .

Still baffled? Examine the content closely. It is a rather inflated call to universal brotherhood which somewhat sniffily proposes that 'this land' is the one and only country on the planet which boasts a benign and humane government, and that it is our mission to spread that good influence to the rest of the world.

Here are two more clues: the poem is always sung rather than read, and lines four to six contain rather lumpy rhymes ending on unstressed syllables, and that also occurs in the well-known first stanza. The extract has an old-fashioned feel about it, and in fact the anonymous author penned it in the mid 1800s. Think of the tune, and you may jump to the answer. Or, if you want one more final clue, stand up rather than jump.

Just a reminder: the answers to this and the following poems are in Appendix two.

Poem two

The next teaser is just as famous, but the subject matter is quite different. The link between the two is that you will have heard both being sung rather than spoken or read in the privacy of an anthology.

These words come from a hymn, then, but before you complain that you don't know any hymns, here is a real giveaway clue. This one is usually heard on every Christmas Eve:

> For He is our childhood's pattern;
> Day by day, like us He grew;
> He was little, weak and helpless,
> Tears and smiles like us He knew;
> And He feeleth for our sadness,
> And He shareth in our gladness.

There's a pretty obvious clue in the fact that each pronoun describing the subject of the poem begins with a capital letter ('He', not 'he'), which is the way that Jesus is referred to. Do you want an even bigger clue? It is traditionally sung *a capella* (without accompaniment) by a solo boy chorister in a Cambridge college service on Christmas Eve.

Poem three

The next stanza comes from a poem in which it's not the first lines which are famous. It is universally known by its eleventh stanza. Here is stanza two:

> The sea was wet as wet could be,
> The sands were dry as dry.
> You could not see a cloud, because
> No cloud was in the sky:
> No birds were flying overhead —
> There were no birds to fly.

The first thing that strikes me is the almost excessive simplicity of the lines and the offbeat logic. Of course, you cannot see clouds if there are none, and of course the sea is wet. In fact, the language is so bland that it is not easy to determine where it originates from.

The one strong clue is that the last two lines have a surreal feel to them. In addition, the directness of the whole could signify that the poem is written for children. It also contains an element of weird humour about it, which is typical of this writer.

A final clue: the author's real name is Charles Lutwidge Dodgson, and the Wikipedia entry for his pen-name coyly suggests that critics cannot agree whether his interest in children, including one particular young girl, had 'an erotic component'. (Gosh, surely not.)

Poem four

And next in this selection, here comes a stanza from a poem from which I reckon just about everybody knows the first verse, particularly if you have studied English poetry a little:

> Can storied urn or animated bust
> Back to its mansion call the fleeting breath?
> Can Honour's voice provoke the silent dust,

Or Flatt'ry soothe the dull cold ear of Death?

Poetry can be quite compressed in meaning and this is a case in point. One clue suggests these lines were written in the nineteenth century or before, and that is the capitalisation of words which personify – in this case – ideas rather than concrete objects or people: 'Honour', 'Flattery' and 'Death'.

The first couplet in particular has a great deal of meaning squeezed into it. A 'storied urn' means a commemorative chalice on which the events of a life are recorded, but neither that or a life-like bust of the deceased can bring them back to their privileged lives in their mansions or country houses.

If you ponder a moment on the first line, you should come up with a clue as to the famous setting of the poem. A 'storied urn' and an 'animated bust', together with the references to death and the transience of life indicate that this poem is set in a graveyard, where an urn and bust cannot breathe life in the person buried there, and in fact the first word of the poem's title is 'Elegy', a recollection and reflection on death.

Poem five

And finally, here is a trickier challenge. This involves detective work of a different kind. Here the clue to the author lies in the subject-matter as well as the leaden pomposity of the lines. If you have read *Making Sense of Poetry* volume one you will have come across the poet's name before. If not, I offer a clue after the quote.

In his posthumously published 'The Temple of Nature' (1803), this scientist writes of how:

> Organic life beneath the shoreless waves
> Was born and nurs'd in Ocean's pearly caves;
> First forms minute, unseen by spheric glass,
> Move on the mud, or pierce the watery mass;
> These, as successive generations bloom,
> New powers acquire, and larger limbs assume;

> Whence countless groups of vegetation spring,
> And breathing realms of fin and feet and wing.

In the line containing the word 'minute' (meaning small rather than sixty seconds of time), the rather odd turn of phrase 'spheric glass' implies that these forms are too tiny to be observed under a microscope.

If the last couple of lines cause you trouble, they signify that these evolving life forms which grow in size and complexity from one generation to the next did so at first in water, where there are many different kinds of vegetation, and the last line implies that they can also become 'breathing', in other words they crawl out of the water on to the shore, grow legs and some fly in the air.

These words were penned with all the pomp and circumstance of the nineteenth century and its preoccupation with progress and the irresistible onward march of science.

The biggest clue goes like this: the writer had a very famous grandson who was responsible for developing and publishing the ideas in those lines above for which he was much praised at the time for their innovative content. As the Americans would say, Go figure. Or, failing that, go to Appendix two.

In our next interlude, we turn to a much more complicated challenge, but first, a poem from a contemporary poet.

Chapter two – Getting up early

The poem is entitled 'Early riser' and it's by Robert Saxton, a favourite of mine amongst modern poets:

> To greet the dawn you needn't step outside.
> With curtains open, savour your living room –
> the stillness of a just-discovered tomb,
> the furniture patient at the light's low tide,
>
> the muted recollection of a friend
> who blessed your evening. Only shapes are left
> but colours will soon seep back: this is no theft,
> merely the loan that all of us extend
>
> to our planetary nature every night.
> Although each reinstatement brings us less,
> the softness calms us, cushioning our distress,
> the tax of time on even so short a flight.
>
> So: over breakfast, plan the day's campaigns –
> your losses have gone unnoticed, like your gains.

First of all, you probably counted the lines and yes, it's another sonnet. That's the characteristic the poem shares with the Shakespeare example. This underlines my point about reading poetry widely, as the knowledge gained by studying Shakespeare's sonnet can be fruitfully applied in this case.

In particular, note the concept that the sonnet sets out a question, discusses it, and at the end comes to a conclusion of some kind. You will see that the final couplet begins 'So:' to highlight that fact. What a shame that 'so' has been hijacked by everyone from social media influencers to every interviewee on the telly nowadays. Sparingly used, it's quite a powerful little word.

Looking at the way the poem is set out, you may notice at least two different aspects of it from Shakespeare's: first, it is divided into three quatrains (four-line stanzas), which rhyme ABBA, and one couplet at the end.

The poem's title, our next item for investigation, is 'Early Riser'. On a basic level, it is a fitting description of someone getting up first thing, but it may conceal much more than that. Quite often, titles only tell part of the story in the poem, but they are still a valuable entrance point to an understanding of it.

Next, you will probably have seen that there is one more interesting visual feature in the poem. Consider the first words of each line, and you will see that only some of them are capitalised, namely, when the first word of a line is also the first word of a sentence. It's a common feature of contemporary poetry and there is no law, poetic or otherwise, which decrees that each line should begin with a capital letter.

There is even an experimental American poet, e. e. cummings, as he liked to style his name, who espoused lower case throughout a poem, including for the first person singular. (Google his name online to see what some of his poetry looks like.)

Capitalising the first word of a line is a custom, rather than a directive from Poetry Central, and one which has worked well in the past, where you will find a majority of end stop lines, that is, where the meaning or part of it is contained within a line. Another aspect of capitalisation to take note of is that in older poetry where personification of concrete and abstract objects occur the word referring to them is set with an initial upper case (like Honesty, Courage, Beauty, and so on).

In other words, not capitalising the first word of a line signifies that the meaning is more important than the rhythmic pattern of the verse and helps to take 'Poetry' down a peg, to break down the barriers between poetry and prose, rendering it more approachable and more self-effacing. The practice of running sense on from one line to the next is known by the French term 'enjambement' (from 'enjamber', to step or stride over), and employing a lower case initial where this appears can make the text flow more fluidly, as in this poem:

> Only shapes are left
> but colours will soon seep back

There is another point to be made here which is hidden in the opening couplet of the poem. Speak it out loud to see if you can determine what I am trying to explain:

> To greet the dawn you needn't step outside.
> With curtains open, *savour* your living room

I have italicised the word which leaps out from the page, for me at least. Poetry tends to be written with a particular rhythm in mind, but here the gentle deviations from the norms of iambic pentameters or whatever lend the poem a certain informality and authenticity.

What is going on here? Let's assume Saxton had written the first line one of these ways:

> With curtains open, *smell* your living room *or*
> With curtains open, *taste* your living room

Can you see what has happened? Two things have changed: first, the alternative lines both fit the rhythm, but secondly, the meaning has been subtly shifted to refer only to one of the senses instead of 'savour' which has a much broader connotation, involving taste, sight and sound, and possibly touch, too.

In addition, there is a suggestion of pleasurable recall in the word 'savour'. The fact that it makes the pattern of the line slightly awkward indicates that Saxton is more concerned with communicating than with crafting the poem as a clever virtuoso performance for a special elite. That is an example of what I referred to in the Introduction under 'rhythm and rhyme' – a metrical variation which strikes the reader, and which is easily noticeable with practice. You will also notice the dissonance between the formal division of the sonnet into two initial quatrains and the way in which the meaning of the poem runs across them.

At this point, you may be posing a question which it is not an easy matter to answer. Did the poet really mean to do that? One of the less quixotic modern attempts to reshape literary analysis, called New Criticism, calls this the 'intentional fallacy'. In case you are wondering, I believe the daftest attempt is Rezeptionsasthetik, analysing a work by its reception. My own view, for what it is worth, bumbling eclecticism is always the best approach, or to put it more simply, use what works, discard what doesn't.

Let me explain: the 'intentional fallacy' refers to giving due weight to what you think the poet intended by the poem under the microscope. The problem with that challenge is that you don't know what the poet intended, and in any case you are asking the wrong question. The poet produces the poem – and the interaction between the poem and you, the reader, depends on a whole number of factors. Here's one: when was the poem written and how old are you, the reader?

Take, for example, the phrase 'just-discovered tomb' in line 3. Most readers with a Christian background will note the reference to Easter Day and the tomb of Christ which, when opened, was found to be empty. Or, if you have a traditional education and count, like me, three score years and ten (and a bit), you will probably also hear echoes of Tutankhamun's tomb and the egyptologist Howard Carter.

Or neither of the above. You still can recognise the concept and significance of an empty tomb which somehow retains the aura of the former life of the man or woman for whom it was constructed. The nature of the impact of that phrase depends as much on your own life experiences and knowledge as it does what the poet may or may not have 'intended' to say.

The point of view is that of the second person. You, the reader, are drawn into the experience directly.

As it is a sonnet, let's explore the conclusion which Saxton arrives at. This poem is all about the past, present and future. Yesterday a well-loved guest occupied the room, but now only his/her aura remains. You can take a moment as an early riser to look both backwards, savouring with pleasure rather than regret, and forwards to the even tenor of another day.

It does not promise eternal life to that experience, unlike Shakespeare who claims to do so through the medium of his art, it simply states that in most lives, one day is very much like another and all we should do is to face each day as it comes. A variation on that much copied poster caption from World War Two comes to mind: Keep calm and carry on reading poetry.

When I first saw this poem printed in the *Spectator*, I was immediately captivated by two things: the use of language and imagery, and secondly the entirely unpretentious nature of its message. For a novice interpreter of poetry, this is an accessible modern poem, and the longer you spend on it the more rewarding it becomes.

Interlude two – Name these poems

In this interlude, I present you with a much more challenging exercise. Instead of listing for you lesser-known stanzas from a familiar poem, hymn, etc, I have for you an interesting quatrain (four liner). The source of this challenge goes back to the days when Radio 4 bore its original name of the Home Service and it broadcast a programme called 'Round Britain Quiz', which featured a whole range of mind-bending challenges. One of the most famous of these was the question which presented a four-line 'stanza', each line pilfered from a different source.

The task before you is that each of the lines in the quatrain below comes from a work by a separate poet, and you have to try and identify the poet and the poem from which it is taken. I do not expect you to name any or all of the poets, just try and get as far as you can using the clues in the lines of verse before you. Here is my own home-grown offering for you to unscramble:

> Thy hair soft-lifted by the winnowing wind
> Which alters when it alteration finds:
> Times wingéd chariot hurrying near –
> This bed thy center is, these walls, thy spheare.

That pretty incoherent mashup teases you to determine as much as possible about the source of each line, and to nail the author and poem wherever possible. There are clues aplenty and it's up to you to determine what they signify. If you don't want some clues, look away now.

Line one:
This is a little tricky if you are not familiar with the poem itself, but the unusual descriptor 'soft-lifted' hints at the writer. A lot of lyric poetry features bucolic scenes and the phrase 'winnowing wind' gives the game away, in that this was a task performed long before someone invented the combine harvester. Winnowing was

the removing of chaff from grain with a fork or other implement, using the wind as the separator. The other famous ode by this poet was addressed to a Grecian urn. Forgive the awful pun, but that poem is one in which every pitcher tells a story. No, I haven't just forgotten how to spell.

Line two:
This is the line lifted from a well-known sonnet. Sorry about the almost rhyme at the end of the line, but in mitigation, 'wind' and 'find' are often paired in poetry of previous centuries, famously in 'Blow, blow thou Winter wind, thou art not so unkind...' (Shakespeare, *As you Like It*.)

Line three:
The accent indicates the adjective is to be pronounced as two syllables. Time is personified as a chariot rushing along and anxious to wipe out this fleeting moment. The theme of the transience of love and happiness is a very common one in lyric poetry, namely, that of the uncertain nature of life combined with the poet's longing to make this precious moment endure.

Line four:
This is an aubade, a poem about dawn, which seeks to make the passing early daylight moment last for longer, since the whole world is encompassed by the space of the lovers' bed. The antique spelling 'spheare' indicates that this line was penned way back in a past century, and the reference is to Ptolemaic cosmology (if that helps). The use of 'center' is also archaic.

Just to let you know: the answers are to be found in Appendix two.

Chapter three – Anna Barbauld and the mystery building

Now I have a real teaser for you. Written by a nineteenth-century woman poet who rejoiced in the name of Anna Laetitia Barbauld, these lines present you with a fascinating conundrum to resolve. She is addressing a poem to a stranger visiting an unusual edifice, and your task is to try and determine what on earth she may be directing these laudatory words towards.

I quote the first chunk of the poem, addressed to a 'stranger', a passer-by who is invited to pause and consider this unusual construction. The title of the poem, with the keyword blanked out by me, is 'Inscription for an Xxx-Xxxxx'. (So it isn't an ode to a public lavatory, but it is still pretty unusual).

I am already giving you a minor clue in that the mystery object begins with a vowel, otherwise the title would be 'Inscription for a Xxx-Xxxxx'. This double-barrelled name can also be spelled out as two separate words. Here is the extract for you to consider:

> Stranger, approach! within this iron door
> Thrice locked and bolted, this rude arch beneath
> That vaults with ponderous stone the cell; confined
> By man, the great magician, who controuls
> Fire, earth, and air, and genii of the storm,
> And bends the most remote and opposite things
> To do him service and perform his will, –
> A giant sits; stern Winter, here he piles,
> While summer glows around, and southern gales
> Dissolve the fainting world, his treasured snows
> Within the rugged cave. Stranger approach!

Note the odd spelling of 'controls' in the fourth line; that is simply an archaic version of the word. The capitalisation of 'Winter' near the end, followed by 'summer' in lower case, is probably a mistake. As personifications, they should both be capitalised. Note that there are no rhyming words at the end of lines.

This is called 'blank verse', the most famous exponent of which was Shakespeare. It is so successful because it follows the natural rhythms of the English language in iambic pentameters. Note how the iambic pentameter deals with awkward words which do not fit the unstressed, stressed pattern: 'ponderous' squeezes three syllables into that foot, so to speak, and it hardly causes a ripple on the surface of the line.

I assume that our previous encounters with the adjective 'rude' already will cause you no problems with line 2. Placing the word 'beneath' after the word it refers to is a common poetic device of the time.

A typical stylistic conceit employed in the century in which this poem appeared (but not exclusively then) is a device which in the wrong hands can at times be irritating. It opens with an eleven-line sentence in which the subject and verb are postponed right up until the eighth line: 'A giant sits'. In the right hands, as here with the opening words of John Milton's *Paradise Lost*, this technique is both powerful and compelling:

> Of Man's First Disobedience, and the Fruit
> Of that Forbidden Tree, whose mortal taste
> Brought Death into the World, and all our woe,
> With loss of *Eden*, till one greater Man
> Restore us, and regain the blissful Seat,
> Sing Heav'nly Muse...

The main clause verb 'sing' is postponed until the sixth line and the impact is all the greater. Those two are examples of Position and Style which I referred to earlier as one of my twelve commandments.

You may well be puzzled by the singing muse in the last line of the Milton quote. This is a reference to the Classical Greek muses, goddesses of which there were nine in all, each of whom is dedicated to a form of the poetic and musical arts. They were invoked in order to bring inspiration to the poet. Calliope was the muse of lyric poetry, and the oddly-named Terpsichore the muse of dancing. Again, these are Classical references which you will come across frequently in such poems.

One more comment: the object which the stranger is enjoined to investigate is a kind of building, the first of which were constructed in the seventeenth century, and which only the richest families could afford. It would be built away from the main house and often would be partly or wholly underground.

Now for a look at the word fields in the poem. The first to strike the reader is the reference in the title to this building constructed for a practical use rather than a mixture of the aesthetically pleasing and purely practical, unlike a glass orangery. There are two phrases at the head of this word field, the first being the words of the title, which actually appear nowhere in the body of the poem, but it is apparently synonymous with the words 'the rugged cave' in the last line of the extract.

The other principal word field relates to the seasons of summer and winter, which are somehow key to the use to which this mysterious edifice is put. It seems that the rugged cave is somehow insulated from the heat of summer and the cold of winter.

Here are some more hints if you are still mystified. The nearest to a 'give-away', should you require it, comes in the latter part of the extract, where again the normal word order of a sentence is stood on its head: 'here he piles … his treasured snows within the rugged cave'. 'He' is Winter, personified with the initial capital letter.

Remember that this is a practical building used until the early twentieth century in the richest houses. Less affluent households could purchase an identical product from the back of a horse-drawn cart.

Three final easy clues coming up: the building is usually at its emptiest towards the end of autumn, and at its fullest in early spring. Secondly, the stranger would be well advised, when entering this building, to wear sturdy shoes, an overcoat and a pair of gloves. And one more clue: the second last line contains the word 'snows' – that might be a hint of the purpose and contents of the building. and if it isn't, the answer is at the end of Appendix two.

Chapter four – the death of Heraclitus

Now for a very straightforward poem which you might well skim through and think that there isn't a great deal to it, but it really does have hidden depths. I came across it when I was a student and was immediately captivated by its blend of grief and positivity. It is a translation by William Cory, a nineteenth-century teacher at Eton, who lost his post there after what was coyly described as an 'indiscreet letter' from himself to a pupil was brought to light.

His only other less dubious claim to fame was this poem, a translation of an epitaph to a Greek poet. When you read it, imagine you have been asked to write say 700 words about it. How would you go about such a task?

> They told me, Heraclitus, they told me you were dead,
> They brought me bitter news to hear and bitter tears to shed.
> I wept as I remembered how often you and I
> Had tired the sun with talking and sent him down the sky.
>
> And now that thou art lying, my dear old Carian guest,
> A handful of grey ashes, long, long ago at rest,
> Still are thy pleasant voices, thy nightingales, awake;
> For Death, he taketh all away, but them he cannot take.

At first glance there does not appear to be much to say about it, but look closer and examine the poem line by line. Your objective when reading an unseen poem like this is to act as a detective, if you like, taking all the clues in the text and forming an overall conclusion based on them. Here comes my attempt at meeting that challenge.

First, it is an untitled two-stanza work with the rhyming pattern AA, BB. The first two lines tell us that this is a lament for Heraclitus. Next, there is a half clue that this may have been penned in the nineteenth century (or before), because of the use of the old form 'taketh' in the last line. As well as ensuring that the metrical patterns in the line run smoothly – 'for Death, he takes all things away' is a bit lame in contrast – it is a formal use of the verb with religious overtones, and this is entirely appropriate here.

Note too that 'Death' is accorded an initial capital. In the nineteenth century and earlier, it was common to capitalise abstract terms which are personified, as I noted earlier. Let me translate that into English: words like Death, Beauty, Honour, Disgust and so on were often treated as if they were living beings, so to speak. Overlooking the fact that it is a little hard to regard Death as a living being, this capitalisation of abstract nouns is a guide to their function in a poem.

Incidentally, did you notice that there is another personification in the poem: in the last line of the first stanza, the sun is treated as if it were a person. I refuse to get into a pillow fight with the woke community as to the appropriate gender for the sun, being here masculine. It is a neat concept that the friends' conversations almost literally went on for so long that the sun, tired of being up there in the sky, was driven to his/her/its rest by them.

If you now recall that much lyric poetry takes a particular person, relationship or incident and generalises it in some way, you will see that this is precisely what occurs in these two stanzas. The first relates the grief of the writer for the death of Heraclitus (of whom more in a moment), and the second generalises it to state that while he is now cremated and turned to ashes, his poetry, like the song of nightingales, will never die.

More often than not, a description of the passionate relationship between two lovers both recognises that they as individuals will not last for ever, but also that their love has been so powerful that it will never die, as it will live on in the poet's writings. Look no further than Shakespeare's sonnets for proof of that, as we did in Chapter one.

If you are curious about the name and place name – Heraclitus and Caria – a few moments alone with Wikipedia will resolve those issues. Search for 'William Cary'.

One interesting question is: did you recognise that this is in fact a translation? There are just a couple of half clues I have noticed, having in the past translated some German poetry myself. The very first line contains a repeated clause: 'they told me', but it fits so neatly into rhythm of the verse that it is hardly noticeable that this is a filler, as it were, making up the verbal patterns of the line.

The same can be said of the repetition of 'long' in the second line of the second stanza. As translations go, this is a pretty good one.

On the whole, it's a polished piece of craftsmanship,, evocative and genuine-sounding, with just the right leavening of poetic techniques – personification and, in particular, the notion of poems as 'nightingales' whose song soars to the heavens – to make it a truly memorable read.

And, just for the record, I have just slipped under the word limit I imposed: 678 words about a poem which at first sight looks too straightforward to require comment is not that bad.

Interlude three – The language of the past

One of the key challenges of reading the poetry of past generations is the need to bear in mind that, the further you go back over the centuries, the more two significant changes take place: first, the language is at a different point of evolution, and secondly, the technologies and social context which are dominant at the time are far from the same in character. Each brings with it a diversity of vocabulary which at times can be daunting.

Let me translate that fairly inscrutable sentence with a couple of examples. Wind back to the days of Queen Victoria and you will soon recognise that the world then was a very different place. Take travel for instance. The internal combustion engine was still waiting to become the dominant means of transport and instead the horse was the principal means of getting about in and between towns and cities, and also for farming in the countryside.

Not only did it cause massive pollution issues from what one riding school I saw called the 'end product' of their animals, it generated a swathe of vocabulary in every aspect of society. In shipping, the shift from sail to steam was accelerating, and the railways were coming to take over from the canal system. The railways, incidentally, helped to unify the country by standardising clock time, so that transport over distance could run to a uniform timetable.

Huge social changes were also taking place, such as compulsory schooling introduced in the latter part of the century; and the first communications revolution was under way with the electric telegraph and the telephone. Also, the nineteenth century was an age of much scientific progress and a faith in its power to create future social advances.

As you will gather, this is an enormous subject, and I can do no more than make you broadly aware of the social and cultural context in which poets of the nineteenth and other centuries were writing.

Here is a random test of nineteenth-century words and

their context. See how many you can work out without resorting to Google, Wikipedia or online dictionaries. Answers will be found in Appendix three:

phrenology	ostler
balaclava	blue stocking
telegraph	bags o' mystery
married to Brown Bess	peelers and bobbies
daguerrotype	
furlong	dray
phaeton	mantle
parts his hair with a towel	bone shaker

Chapter Five – Total nonsense?

Now for a different kind of challenge. Here is part of a poem which was dismissed for years as 'nonsense', but it does contain a good deal of sense, if only it were approached from the right direction. Honest. Read it through a couple of times and see what you make of it, before I get going on trying to analyse it with you:

> woe our good kaspar is dead.
> who's going to bear the burning banner in his pigtail, who's going to turn the coffee-mill, who's going to entice the idyllic deer.
> …
> now our heads and our toes are shrivelling up and the fays lie half charred on the funeral pyres, now the black bowling alley is thundered behind the sun and there is no one left to wind up the compasses and cartwheels.
> who's going to eat with the rat now at the solitary table, who's going to chase away the devil when he tries to lead the horses astray, who's going to explain to us the monograms in the stars.
> his bust will grace the fireplaces of all truly noble men but that is small consolation and snuff for a death's head.

This is part of my translation of a poem by the Dadaist poet and sculptor Hans Arp, most recently published in 2003 in the *Music while drowning* anthology of Expressionist poems for Tate Publishing.

The reason I have selected this tough challenge for you is to make a couple of points about 'difficult' poems, of which this is surely one. When I first came across Arp's poetry in the 1960s, I was a junior lecturer in a University German department, and when I asked around about his work I was told it was nonsense poetry, and that's just about all there is to it.

It struck me that it was rather odd that total nonsense

should have any place in the Hall of Fame of German poetry, and I also sensed that his work was not nonsense at all. All you have to do is to look at it with different eyes, so to speak. The first point is that so-called nonsense has a long and significant role to play in the history of poetry, not least in rhymes for children:

> Hey, diddle, diddle, the cat and the fiddle
> The cow jumped over the moon
> The little dog laughed to see such craft
> And the dish ran away with the spoon.

The alternative end word in the second last line – craft – I prefer because it makes for an internal rhyme (laughed, craft). There is a power about this language which has nothing to do with 'meaning', but it does possess an inner integrity – it sort of makes sense on its own terms, and demonstrates the power of language which does not necessarily make complete logical sense.

And so does a novel like *Alice in Wonderland*, which has its own internal structural integrity. Like the game of cricket: to an alien, it appears to be an absurd antiquated ritual conducted solely by posh men in white, but if you get 'inside' it the whole thing does make sense, even though the details may remain obscure. So let's not confuse 'nonsense' with pure 'randomness', which does not make sense, except entirely by chance.

Let me offer you a prize example from another German poet, Christian Morgenstern, famous for his satirical poems. In 'The impossible Fact', his comical character Palmström is run over by a lorry. He digs into the local law books and discovers that vehicles were not allowed at that spot and comes to the cheerful conclusion that he must have dreamt the experience, because 'what should not be cannot be'.

Entirely 'nonsensical', but a serious point lies within it, namely, that a certain cast of mind venerates authority more than logic, and it should be exposed and condemned by satirical verse like this.

There have been all manner of different approaches to

Arp's lament for Kaspar, some that the poem is bizarre political satire, but most go along with the overriding conclusion that it is 'just' nonsense. But how do you begin to chip away to reveal the 'meaning' in such a poem? Answer: find one or more bits that do make some sense to you, draw a conclusion from them and see where that takes you. Let me demonstrate.

Read the poem from beginning to end, and I hope you agree that at least it seems to be seeking to make some kind of sense overall, in that because Kaspar is dead, the poet is grieving at his loss, and a whole number of things which are no longer possible. Most of those things are magical, and it's as if Kaspar's death has snuffed out a flame of imagination and inspiration which can no longer be retrieved. The loss of Kaspar has deprived the world of its sense of wonder and insight into the mysteries of the universe.

Now read the poem again, and I hope you will begin to see that it's beginning to appear more coherent. It all revolves around those two concepts: first, that Kaspar is dead and that is a source of overwhelming grief, and secondly, his death means that certain vital activities are no longer possible.

'Snuff for a death's head' is the most accessible of the weird turns of phrase which abound this poem, so it is an indication that what appears to be nonsensical is just something just a little more obscure than normal, and we might be able to winkle open more of the poem with a touch of ingenuity.

Note that the lament for Kaspar points to his powers and abilities which are no longer accessible, now that he is dead. For example, there is now no one able to explain the monograms in the stars, by which is meant the constellations and their interpretation. There is also an indication here that Kaspar had supernatural powers to divine and understand the universe, and that is all blocked off now. In other words, he was a figure who could act as an intermediary between this life and whatever may lie beyond.

Other segments are less easy to disentangle. The line about a burning banner in his pigtail simply brings to mind the images of a girl in traditional Bavarian dress, sporting pigtails and holding a glass of beer and the German flag, often seen in contemporary advertising. And again, back to a line which appears to be an oblique reference to the Revelations of St John the Divine, in the phrase lamenting that there is now no one to chase away the devil. I suspect the reference is to Revelation 12:9:

> And the great dragon was cast out, that old serpent, called the Devil, and Satan, which deceiveth the whole world: he was cast out into the earth, and his angels were cast out with him.

It points to the fact that some of the poem cannot be reduced to facts. But let's take a step back and examine the historical context, which can be invaluable in coming to an understanding of an apparently inscrutable poem. It was written during the First World War, a time which itself, according to the Dadaists, was totally insane, destructive beyond belief and which trashed all the magic and beauty in the world and trampled it in the mindless bloody ritual of trench warfare.

In general terms, Kaspar appears to signify a figure of innocence who helped to make sense of the world, and that with his death innocence and meaning are sucked out entirely. It could be a Garden of Eden reference, or to a particular innocent creature who has appeared in our society untainted by civilisation and is then struck down.

There is another external clue in this poem, which would be familiar to Germans and others, too, and that lies in the name of Kaspar. Like Mowgli, the jungle boy of Rudyard Kipling, brought up by a pack of wolves, the historical Kaspar Hauser was brought up in the wild.

He turned up in Nuremberg in Bavaria in 1830, claiming to have lived away from civilisation. He was regarded as a symbol of innocence, despite claims that he may have been a fraud. Imagine what a kerfuffle there would be nowadays on

Twitter and Instagram if a Kaspar appeared in our midst.

It is of course not always possible to determine the date and provenance of an unseen poem which you are required to study, but there may be internal clues which could give you a general idea. Also, do not worry if you haven't 'cracked' every last phrase in the poem, as some may be purely fanciful.

Or they may be obscure references that you do not recognise. For example, the 'bimbam' in line one equates to the English ding, dong. So it could refer to bells tolling at his demise. But it is not essential for you to pick up every allusion, and remember that applies to poems which are not 'nonsense', too. You will not be able to understand every reference, but you will gain an overall picture if you persevere.

But before I go any further, the reason I have been going into such detail with the Arp poem is that if you come across a 'difficult' poem of any kind, you can apply the same techniques to chip away at the sense and significance of it. Find something that sort of makes sense to you and use that as a lever to force open the secrets inside. I tend to work on the principle that the poet actually wishes to communicate something to his/her readers, and if that does not happen, it could well be the poet's fault, not yours.

Chapter six – Religious fervour

Now for a real tough nut, a poet – Gerard Manley Hopkins – who has partly invented his own language to express the feelings and visions he has in the almost fanatical intensity of his Catholic faith, which makes a lot of his stuff less than accessible at first sight.

These two stanzas are an extract from *The Wreck of the Deutschland*, a ship in which five Franciscan nuns perished. Here he is expressing his faith. Do remember that though this may not be your kind of subject, we are here to interpret a poem, not to deal with our own religious and other feelings or beliefs or to comment on those of the poet:

> I am soft sift
> In an hourglass – at the wall
> Fast, but mined with motion, a drift,
> And it crowds and combs to the fall;
> I steady as water in a well, to a poise, to a pane,
> But roped with, always, all the way down from the tall
> Fells or flanks of the voel, a vein
> Of the gospel proffer, a pressure, a principle, Christ's gift.
>
> I kiss my hand
> To the stars, lovely-asunder
> Starlight, wafting him out of it; and
> Glow, glory in thunder;
> Kiss my hand to the dappled-with-damson west:
> Since, tho' he is under the world's splendour and wonder,
> His mystery must be instressed, stressed;
> For I greet him the days I meet him, and bless when I understand.

That caused a couple of problems for my spell-checker. The first is an obscure term – 'voel' – for bald, here in its extended sense of a bare hill-top. The second is 'instressed', which is one of

Hopkin's idiosyncratic formulations that pepper his poems. Some work better than others. Here is a fine typical example of his powerfully compressed language:

As a dare-gale skylark scanted in a dull cage

I still find 'instressed' a bit of a conundrum. If you are still struggling with the meaning of the above line, the skylark, used to flying free and challenge the wind is held tightly prisoner in the scant confines of the dull and unstimulating cage. More about instressed in a minute.

Now let me turn in more detail to the extract before you. The language is highly compressed and will take a while to disentangle. The strange but powerful metaphor of himself in an hourglass, where the grains inside hold fast at the wall, in other words near the glass, but in the middle everything is sliding down in a fall (or Fall, perhaps?). This, like the fourth line onwards, is similar in meaning, describing the steadiness of water in a well which is always at risk of being roped up into the air above.

The next verse praises the creation of heaven and earth in the paradoxical mercifulness and violence of the universe. Note another hugely compressed phrase in 'dappled-with-damson west', referring to the sun sinking at sunset.

God is present in all things, argues this stanza, which is the meaning he probably assigns to 'instressed'. These stanzas encapsulate the paradoxes of Christ's suffering and those of Man struggling to come to terms with religious belief. Whatever your own religious convictions or none, the poem is worth reading because of the sheer majesty of the manner in which the poet takes the English language by the scruff of the neck and compresses complex concepts into a highly-charged turn of phrase.

His poetry is an acquired taste, perhaps, but once you have begun to recognise what he is trying to express in such powerful compacted terms, you may want to read more.

Chapter seven – Broken statue in the desert

The next poem up for analysis is *Ozymandias,* a famous work by Shelley. To put you all out of your misery (including me), the name is a variant on the much more familiar Rameses II, the ancient Egyptian Pharaoh. Read it through carefully a couple of times and decide how you should go about unlocking its meaning:

Ozymandias

I met a traveller from an antique land
Who said: 'Two vast and trunkless legs of stone
Stand in the desert . . . Near them, on the sand,
Half sunk, a shattered visage lies, whose frown
And wrinkled lip, and sneer of cold command,
Tell that its sculptor well those passions real
Which yet survive, stamped on these lifeless things,
The hand that mocked them, and the heart that fed:
And on the pedestal these words appear:
"My name is Ozymandias, king of kings:
Look on my works, ye Mighty, and despair!
Nothing beside remains. Round the decay
Of that colossal wreck, boundless and bare
The lone and level sands stretch far away.'

Looking at the shape of the poem, it is definitely a sonnet in form. The title of the poem is of no great help, hinting at a past name of some significance, perhaps, and the first three lines indicate that the subject is a huge statue which now lies broken in the desert. The punctuation indicates that the bulk of the poem is the account by a traveller from 'an antique land', Ancient Egypt as it turns out.

The metrical form is that of the iambic pentameter which we have encountered before and the sentence with the exclamation mark indicates that this is a high point of some kind in the narrative.

There are four personalities in this sonnet: the narrator (first person), the traveller who does all the speaking, the ancient Pharaoh himself, whose likeness lies scattered on the 'lone and level sands'. then, on line 6, the sculptor of the statue appears.

Ozymandias, it appears, was not a particularly pleasant individual. He wielded supreme power with a 'sneer of cold command'. He even gets a speaking part in the form of the legend on the statue's pedestal in lines 10-11.

That overweening self-glorification falls apart in the next line with the words 'Nothing beside remains': just a head and legs, broken by the ravages of time, and the pedestal. The sculptor is praised in line 8 for his work, and note that here 'mocked' is used in its less usual meaning of imitated rather than poured scorn on. The word 'fed' is applied in the sense of 'inspires'.

The whole poem depicts the way in which the power and the glory of man is reduced by nature to rubble and decay. Nothing more remains of the sculpture than these few broken pieces, and nothing remains of Rameses II himself at all. His fate is isolation and being forgotten in the vast sands.

One thing puzzles me, and that is why this huge sculpture was constructed in the middle of the desert in the first place. Perhaps the changing climate meant that in the distant past this was a source of adequate water supply and moderate temperatures, and the civilisation itself has also been swept away by the merciless onward march of nature.

Interlude four – External references

A previous interlude tested you on a handful of terms from a past era in our civilisation, and this time we turn to words from a more distant past, everything from Classical Greece and Rome to China and the Bible. This time you can just sit back and absorb the first part of what follows. Challenges to your brain power come after the first pair of warm-up entries.

Morpheus

Here's a line from my favourite Keats's poem *St Agnes Eve*:

> Oh for some drowsy Morphean amulet!

An amulet is a charm to ward off unpleasant things like illness and spells cast against you, and Morphean is the adjectival form of Morpheus, God of sleep and dreams. And, yes, it has been borrowed to apply to the drug morphine. However, there is an inner riddle here. Porphyro the youth is keen to seduce and carry Madeleine away from the nasty folk who keep her in the castle against her will.

My question is: if an amulet guards *against* something, and he is yearning for a Morphean amulet, surely he is after a charm which induces sleep on her part? But who am I to challenge the logic of Keats.

Orpheus

Funny thing, language. Take Morpheus and chop off the first letter, and you have a quite different person.
Here is a clue to his powers from Shakespeare's Henry VIII:

> Orpheus with his lute made trees,

And the mountain tops that freeze,
Bow themselves when he did sing:

Orpheus was a demi-God who could with his lyre capture the attention of all men, every living creature and even nature itself. He is also the husband of Eurydice who died when bitten by a snake. He pursued her to the Underworld and was allowed by Hades to bring her back to life, on one condition, that he did not turn round to look at her on his path back into the world. Of course, he did and suffered the consequences.

Your turn

Now for what I hope are some less difficult challenges from the past, mostly legendary. The terms may well be familiar to you, and my question in each case is for you to determine how much you can dig out of your brain about them. I'll give you a few words of introduction in each case.

Boreas/ Aquilo, Zephyrus/Favonius, Notus/Auster, Euros/Vulturnus

An interesting quartet, and their number is a helpful clue to their significance. They come from ancient Greece and were Gods of particular natural phenomena. The names adjoining each item are the Roman equivalents. What are they?

The labours of Hercules

This refers to a number of challenges set to Hercules, and you may well have heard the phrase: 'This is a Herculean task'. The question is in four parts: Who was Hercules? Why did he have to perform these tasks? How many were there? What were they?

The island of Lesbos

The name of the island should ring a bell with you, but the question is: What gave it its resonance in modern culture and why?

Sisyphus and Tantalus

These unfortunates are linked together by the roughly similar nature of their punishment.

Nebuchadnezzar

A royal person and a large bottle. Any ideas?

Ming

An eastern dynasty.

Answers will be found in Appendix four.

Chapter eight – Rural plunder

This next poem is quite different from what has gone before. To begin with, it's a lot longer, and far too long in fact to quote in full. Secondly, there is a strong social theme condemning the depopulation of villages as their inhabitants are induced by the rich and powerful to emigrate overseas to seek their fortune.

It's called 'The Deserted Village' by Oliver Goldsmith, and was published in 1770. I am going to focus on just one of the characters, the village schoolmaster. For the whole poem, which is very accessible to a modern audience and well composed, google the title and you will be swamped with a choice of free listings online.

Here comes the extract, which consists of the opening and closing lines of the poem, and sandwiched in between the description of the village schoolmaster:

> Sweet Auburn, loveliest village of the plain,
> Where health and plenty cheared the labouring swain,
> Where smiling spring its earliest visit paid,
> And parting summer's lingering blooms delayed,
> Dear lovely bowers of innocence and ease,
> Seats of my youth, when every sport could please,
> How often have I loitered o'er thy green,
> Where humble happiness endeared each scene!
> ….
>
> There, in his noisy mansion, skill'd to rule,
> The village master taught his little school;
> A man severe he was, and stern to view,
> I knew him well, and every truant knew;
> Well had the boding tremblers learned to trace
> The day's disasters in his morning face;
> Full well they laughed, with counterfeited glee,
> At all his jokes, for many a joke had he:
> Full well the busy whisper circling round,

Conveyed the dismal tidings when he frowned;
Yet he was kind, or if severe in aught,
The love he bore to learning was in fault;
The village all declared how much he knew;
'Twas certain he could write, and cypher too;
Lands he could measure, terms and tides presage,
And ev'n the story ran that he could gauge.
For even tho' vanquished, he could argue still;
While words of learned length and thundering sound,
Amazed the gazing rustics ranged around;
And still they gazed, and still the wonder grew,
That one small head could carry all he knew.
But past is all his fame. The very spot
Where many a time he triumphed, is forgot.
. . . .

Farewell, and O where'er thy voice be tried,
On Torno's cliffs, or Pambamarca's side,
Whether where equinoctial fervours glow,
Or winter wraps the polar world in snow,
Still let thy voice, prevailing over time,
Redress the rigours of the inclement clime;
Aid slighted truth with thy persuasive strain,
Teach erring man to spurn the rage of gain;
Teach him, that states of native strength possest,
Tho' very poor, may still be very blest;
That trade's proud empire hastes to swift decay,
As ocean sweeps the labour'd mole away;
While self-dependent power can time defy,
As rocks resist the billows and the sky.

Let me examine the poem, taking my list of topics for so doing

one at a time.

Shape, title, and pronunciation

A whisker over 430 lines in length, the poem gives an extensive tour of an imaginary village and its past inhabitants. The rhyme scheme is AA, BB, CC, DD etc., in other words these are rhyming couplets in iambic pentameter form, a style used in longer poems for many centuries, way back to Chaucer's *Canterbury Tales*. It comfortably fits the natural pattern of the English language, and the unrhymed version – known as 'blank verse' – is the bedrock for much of Shakespeare's work. He uses a rhymed couplet for powerful effect, as the end of that fairly well-known soliloquy in *Hamlet* demonstrates:

> Out of my weakness and my melancholy,
> As he is very potent with such spirits,
> Abuses me to damn me. I'll have grounds
> More relative than this. The play's the *thing*
> Wherein I'll catch the conscience of the *king*.

The punctuation shows that most of the lines are end-stop, although there is some effective enjambement. The big change in this pattern comes in the last fourteen lines, which form one long sentence, almost a sonnet at the end of the poem, although that is probably coincidental. More of that later.

So much for the physical appearance of 'The Deserted Village'. The title gives away the main theme, but it does not hint at the vehemence of Goldsmith's attack on those responsible for the destruction of a rural community. The punctuation hints at a powerful conclusion to the description of Auburn and those who used to dwell there.

Vocabulary

The language of the poem is direct and unfussy. There is the occasional archaic word, like 'cheared' (for 'cheered') and 'swain' ('countryfolk'). A 'bower' is a secluded spot. More on the vocabulary in the interlude following this chapter.

Imagery

The village is an idealised version of rural life destroyed, and constitutes a powerful symbol of what has happened to the English countryside and its population. You can see this clearly in the closing lines of the poem cited above, where the village is addressed directly.

Point of view

This is a descriptive poem which has a first person narrcator, who walks through the deserted village of his childhood. although that does not intrude much. The other former residents of the village are lovingly described in turn.

Personalities

A sequence of characters who used to live in the village.

Actions

Most of the poem reflects on the people of the past and their wholesome lifestyles before they were uprooted by greedy rich folk.

Senses

Largely vision, but also the gentle sounds of the village at ease after the day's labours.

Position and style

The tirade against the rich at end of the poem, a fitting climax to his outrage at what has happened to sweet Auburn.

Here the tone and vocabulary shift to express his anger at what has happened to this quiet corner of rural life.

Interlude five – 'Deserted Village' words and phrases

Now for a teaser selection of other words and phrases from 'The Deserted Village', which will assist you if you read the whole poem (please do so – it's widely available online), but, if not, you can still bend your brain to the task of interpreting what these eighteenth-century words and phrases signify.

Do not be disheartened if you fail to grasp the complete meaning of these words and phrases – you will always have to meet this challenge when reading poetry of a past age, and most of the time you can make a reasonable shot at the significance, given the context of the poem (rural England) and the surrounding text. Here comes a test challenge:

> And half a tillage stints thy smiling plain

If you are struggling, the context is that of a once prospering village community which has been destroyed by the greedy rich, and this is part of what is left. Working backwards, the 'smiling plain' refers to the sunlit fields surrounding the village. Now the word 'stints'. You will be familiar with it in the adjective 'unstinting' which means 'unalloyed' or without 'reservation'.

The noun 'stint' is probably less useful to us, as 'the worker did his daily stint', meaning 'allotted amount of work' So the probable meaning of 'stints' as a verb is that it 'mars' the smiling plain, and that makes good sense if we move back to the final problematical term, 'tillage'. It's not a misprint for 'village', by the way.

You may be familiar with the verb 'till', meaning to cultivate, plough – and so the entire line signifies something like this: Half a row of tilled soil mars the smiling plain, which it is implied was once cultivated by the inhabitants of the community.

Here's one more teaser. The narrator had intended to

return to Auburn in order to live out his retirement, but the place is now derelict. What he wanted to do was this:

> To husband out life's taper at the close

Here we clearly have a metaphor elucidating what the narrator intended to do. Again, working backwards from the end of the line, the meaning begins to emerge. The 'close' refers to the final period of the narrator's life. Now for 'life's taper'. Remember we are back in the eighteenth century, when coal and wood heated the houses and candles were used for lighting. A 'taper' is a thin candle, often used for lighting larger candles, so the taper's light represents the life remaining to him.

One more phrase to disentangle: 'to husband out' is related to 'husbandry', the management of a household or a farm, something like 'steward'. It has the extended meaning of 'careful management'. So the whole line means: 'To use up prudently the flame of life remaining in my final years.'

That's as much help as you are going to get, and from now on you are flying solo, so to speak. Here's the promised list. Answers are in Appendix four.

choked with sedges	bittern
sate by his fire	vagrant train
the spoiler's hand	rood of ground
glades folorn	humble bowers
sober herd that lowed	the plashy spring
her wintry faggot	mantling bliss
shewed how fields were won	
nut-brown draughts	furze unprofitably gay
Twelve good Rules, the game of Goose	

the black gibbet	distant climes
wild Altama	that horrid shore
matted woods	and kist her...babes
boding tremblers	aught
cypher	read
gauge	cot
slights	spoiler
pants	labour'd mole

Perhaps I have wrenched some of the phrases unkindly out of their context, but keep in mind the overall tale the narrator has to tell, of a village massacred by the dominance of wealthy and influential men whose inhabitants were forced to go abroad in search of a better life. Appendix five has the answers.

Chapter nine – Trailing clouds of glory

I am not sure who earns the wooden spoon as the poet with the worst title for a poem, but a strong contender is Wordsworth's 'Ode: Intimations of Immortality from Recollections of Early Childhood' from which these lines are extracted:

> Our birth is but a sleep and a forgetting:
> The Soul that rises with us, our life's Star,
> Hath had elsewhere its setting,
> And cometh from afar:
> Not in entire forgetfulness,
> And not in utter nakedness,
> But trailing clouds of glory do we come
> From God, who is our home:
> Heaven lies about us in our infancy!
> Shades of the prison-house begin to close
> Upon the growing Boy,
> But he beholds the light, and whence it flows,
> He sees it in his joy;
> The Youth, who daily farther from the east
> Must travel, still is Nature's Priest,
> And by the vision splendid
> Is on his way attended;
> At length the Man perceives it die away,
> And fade into the light of common day.

This is a substantial chunk of unseen poetry to round off this guide with, so let us follow the principles we have been applying throughout.

First, appearance, punctuation and capitalisation. Reading it aloud, it is clear that this is not a regular standardised format for a poem, although you can see that there is some consistency in the rhyming pattern, which features ABAB alternating with AA. In other words, 'forgetting' and 'Star' rhyme with 'setting' and 'afar', followed by two lines rhyming with the last syllable '-ness'.

Next, let's look at punctuation. It seems to be just one single sentence cascading down the page, which could lead us to view this as a single statement carried through to an end. Turning to capitalisation, these are the words set with an initial capital: 'Soul', 'Star', 'God', 'Heaven' (already capitalised as the first word on the line), 'Boy', 'Youth', 'Nature's Priest', and 'Man'. That looks promising for a word field grouping. More of that in a moment.

The title tells us that this is an ode, a general term for a poem addressing someone or something, describing them and often drawing general conclusions from them. The rest of the title demands a deep breath before trying to pick it apart, but it is worth the effort. An intimation is an insight, a suggestion, a hint. Taken as a whole, it means 'hints of eternal life from reflecting on my youngest years'.

Now the vocabulary, and those capitalised nouns: what they describe is a progression from the spirit into birth, life and the process of maturation. However, Wordsworth does not regard this as a positive onward march from childhood ignorance to adult maturity and understanding. Quite the reverse: he is claiming that we come into this life 'trailing clouds of glory', in other words bringing with us into this world remnants of our pre-life condition of oneness with the universe.

As we grow older, 'shades of the prison house' of adulthood close in on the child as it develops, which reminds me to take a look at the imagery in this extract. There are two really striking metaphors, 'trailing clouds of glory' and 'the prison house'.

Everything conspires together to assert that, as we grow, we evolve away from our connection with the universe into the mundane life of the everyday:

At length the Man perceives it die away,

And fade into the light of common day.

What he is striving to do is to re-establish that connection between Man and Nature which life on earth seeks to obliterate, and which the poet can perhaps achieve some insight into and express it in his verses. Elsewhere in this poem he states:

> To me the meanest flower that blows can give
> Thoughts that do often lie too deep for tears.

All he can now manage to do is to gain hints (intimations) of that past connection. As he writes later in the poem:

> Hence in a season of calm weather
> Though inland far we be,
> Our souls have sight of that immortal sea
> Which brought us hither,
> Can in a moment travel thither,
> And see the children sport upon the shore,
> And hear the mighty waters rolling evermore.

In times of quiet contemplation, however far 'inland' we might be, in other words, however disconnected from the infinite, we can faintly perceive it, which he describes in another powerful metaphor as 'that immortal sea' which bore us on to this earth. Children playing on the shore, in other words, in close contact with, the infinite, can still hear 'the mighty waters' of that heritage which becomes ever more eroded, the older they become.

And that is what Wordsworth's famous phrase in the passage cited at the beginning of this chapter 'The child is father of the man' is all about.

A challenge to the notion of original sin, this is Wordsworth proclaiming the original innocence of the infant, and their closeness to God and the universe, which decays as they grow older and 'shades of the prison-house' of adulthood begin to close in. And if there is any fault in failing as an adult to make this connection with the universe, it is his, not that of the world beyond the self.

It's a longish poem – read it through and you will find it is less impenetrable than you thought.

Chapter ten – In conclusion

My apparently ramshackle collection of samples I have given you to analyse as 'unseen poems' has attempted to illustrate as many aspects as possible of my 'twelve commandments', which I examined in detail in the Introduction.

In each case, I have shown how you can use my 'twelve commandments' to pick apart even the most obscure and 'difficult' poems and build up a clear and rewarding interpretation of them. Remember that poetry is a two-way street. It depends on what you bring to it as much as it brings to you. In other words, the more open you become to the poem, the more insights it offers you.

The experience of reading lyric poetry in particular is very far from that of reading a novel, where a sequence of events and the experiences of characters dominate the narrative. In Wordsworth's view, it is a tranquil recollection of the world of nature and its powerful voice. Do not, he argues, listen to the din of science and the modern world, reach back and capture a hint, if nothing more, of our splendid past.

In 'The Tables turned', Wordsworth expresses those insights in these words:

> Sweet is the lore which Nature brings;
> Our meddling intellect
> Mis-shapes the beauteous forms of things: –
> We murder to dissect.

By allowing the intellect to take over our thought processes, we lose sight of the 'beauteous form of things' and by analysing them we destroy them.

One aspect of lyric poetry which should be emphasised here is that it typically starts with an individual or object and ends by extending it in a generalisation. A striking example is the Shakespearean sonnet which began our study of individual poems, where the comparison between the beloved and a series of weather-related objects becomes generalised into love itself and the way in which it can be made to beat death.

If you think back to 'Early Riser' in Chapter two, this is a typical lyric poem in that it pauses in quiet reflection over the previous evening's activities and looks forward to the coming day. Here too there is a low-key sense in which one evening and the next morning are generalised into the experiences of the everyday

After analysing the poem, you have to put your responses down on paper in a cogent and appropriate form. For assistance in doing this, turn to my eBook and paperback *Making Sense of Essay Writing*, which is described in the list of my publications which follow the main text of this book. As I have already indicated, there is a series of seven episodes of a YouTube guide to making sense of poetry, and you have already seen some attractive screen shots in the illustrations accompanying this text.

Saxton arrives at a radically different conclusion from Wordsworth, but both – like all good poets – give us pause for thought and contemplation. That is what poetry should do, and I hope that you have gained more insight and, I hope, a more sympathetic understanding of how it works when you come to explore and write about 'unseen poems'.

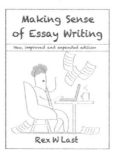

Appendix one – Further reading

My advice here is radically different from what it would have been a couple of decades and more ago. If you want quick access to any poet out of copyright now, simply go online and type your request in the search bar.

If, however, like me you still like to hold a book in your hand, I suggest you find a charity shop near you which has a quality selection of secondhand books on offer. For individual authors, Penguin books are much sought after, but any edition is better than none. The market is awash with modern poets and it would take several lifetimes to read them all.

Anthologies are an excellent way of collecting the best-known poems and it is up to you to find what you can. Penguin produce an excellent anthology of English verse.

Online there is a wealth of choice, and for one-stop shopping, you cannot beat Bartleby.com, a treasure trove of anthologies and the works of individual poets. The 1923 edition of Palgrave's *Golden Treasure* is online too (that is a classic amongst anthologies), and countless other anthologies and poets. Bartelby also figures a large number of classical novels.

Appendix two – Keys to Interludes one and two and Chapter three

Interlude one

Poem one – TheBritish National Anthem

Poem two – Once in Royal David's City

Poem three – Lewis Carroll, *Alice in Wonderland*. Here is the famous bit:

> 'The time has come,' the Walrus said,
> 'To talk of many things:
> Of shoes — and ships — and sealing-wax —
> Of cabbages — and kings —
> And why the sea is boiling hot —
> And whether pigs have wings.'

Poem four – Thomas Gray's 'Elegy in a Country Churchyard'. The famous first stanza runs:

> The curfew tolls the knell of parting day,
> The lowing herd wind slowly o'er the lea,
> The ploughman homeward plods his weary way,
> And leaves the world to darkness and to me.

The 'curfew' is a bell originally telling the population to cover their fires ('couvre' plus 'feu' in French), and knell refers to a passing or death. 'Lowing' means the sound made by cattle. The word 'lea' signifies a stretch of grassland.

Poem five – Erasmus Darwin, 'The Temple of Nature'
Erasmus Darwin was a scientist, slavery abolitionist and proponent of women's education, grandfather of Charles Darwin.

This extract is from his best-known poem on evolutionary processes.

Interlude two

Four poems by four poets, one per line:

Line one – John Keats, 'Ode to Autumn'. Here Autumn itself is addressed. Winnowing was the means of removing the chaff from the grain by raising the mix with a fork to allow the wind to do the necessary separation. Now, of course, combine harvesters cut, thresh and winnow the grain automatically.
Line two – W Shakespeare, Sonnet 116.
Line three – Andrew Marvell, 'To his coy Mistress', where he complains that we do not have a world's worth of time to spend, so let us make love. The metaphor refers to a swiftly-moving vehicle which sweeps away all in its path. In other words, his coy mistress is urged to put aside shyness and hesitancy and respond to his advances.

Note that the weak past participle, here employed as an adjective, used to have the final 'e' pronounced, and if metrical considerations meant that you should not pronounce it, there would usually be an apostrophe in its place like this: 'plac'd'.
Line four – John Donne, 'The Sonne rising', an aubade (poem about the early morning) telling the sun basically to go away and leave us lovers alone. The word 'spheare' is an antique spelling and is a reference to the bed which is the lovers' world and the room itself is like the heavens, which were believed at the time to consist of concentric spheres on which the planets and stars were placed and the earth was at its centre.

Chapter three

The title of the poem is 'The Ice House', a building used to store a year's worth of ice for a large rich household. Many were constructed below ground to help retain the ice over the summer.

Appendix three – Answers to Interlude three

Each of the answers reflects an aspect of Victorian life, some more so than others.

phrenology

This odd term reflects the Victorian preoccupation with appearance and its relationship with good and bad. A strong chin or a bright eye can indicate positive qualities, whilst a shifty look and a limping gait points to criminal proclivities.

One aspect of the human body which was much examined and analysed was the head, and phrenology was the pseudo-science of analysing the patterns, shapes and indentations of the skull to determine character and ethnicity. Different areas of the skull allegedly gave insight into a variety of aspects of human character.

ostler

This is the curious name for a man who looks after horses, usually for visitors at an inn. The word is linked to 'host', 'hospitality'. This item reflects the continuing reliance on the horse for all manner of activities, from acting as a mount to riders, via pulling carriages of various kinds to serving as a beast of burden on a farm or in industry.

balaclava

The nineteenth century, like just about every century, was not without its famous battles and wars, and balaclava refers to an item of headgear which covers all but part of the face. Balaclava is the name of a town near Sebastapol in the Crimea, where war was fought in 1854. The troops wore these knitted garments against the severe cold.

blue stocking

This term referred to women of an intellectual and literary bent and derived from the eighteenth-century Blue Stockings Society. I include this to underline the strong rise of women's activism and search for equality in the Victorian era.

telegraph

In this age, communications became much more rapid and the earliest of these was the telegraph, which evolved into using Morse code (named after its inventor) to send messages over long distances by wire.

bags o' mystery

A slang nineteenth-century reference to sausages. Some cynics may say that not much has changed over the passing decades. Food quality was a serious challenge before the invention of the freezer and refrigerator, and the implication is that various kinds of unorthodox meat were incorporated into the product.

married to Brown Bess

Brown Bess is a term of uncertain origin referring to a self-loading flintlock weapon, and married to her means in the army.

peelers and bobbies

These were the informal names given to the London police force which was created by Sir Robert Peel in the 1820s. In the large cities in particular, law and order was a serious problem.

daguerreotype

Photography was another significant technological advance in the nineteenth century. This name referred to Louis Daguerre who invented one of the early photographic processes.

dray

A horse-drawn cart for carrying barrels of beer, underlining the importance in industry and farming of the heavy horse, one of the most famous of which was the Suffolk Punch. The word dray comes from Old English 'to drag, draw'.

furlong

You do not have to travel far back in time for a whole different world of measurements, from temperature to volume, weight and, here, to linear distance. A furlong comes from the term for the length of a ploughed field, a 'furrow long'. You will come across many such references to old forms of measurement.

mantle

A reminder of the fact that the technology used in Victorian days for lighting and heating was gas, and the mantle was a ceramic mesh which the gas when lit would turn bright enough to light a room. As I recall, it was about the level of a 40 watt bulb in my grandmother's house.

phaeton

There were a large number of horse-driven vehicles of various shapes and sizes, and one website counts around 70-odd types, including everything from a diligence to a gig. The phaeton was the improbable name of a light carriage, usually with two seats. The word goes back to an ancient term for 'light', via the Phaethon, son of Helios, the sun God. In his youth, Phaethon persuades his father to let him drive the chariot of sun through the sky. He causes catastrophic damage, and was possibly the world's first bad driver. The insurance claim must have been enormous.

Another important type of horse-drawn vehicle was the charabanc, which had a motorised descendant of the same name. That is yet another example of a French word which has sneaked its way into English. It means a carriage with benches, and did not offer any protection against the elements. Two more charming names for horse-drawn vehicles I found were Meadowbrook and Sulky.

bone shaker

For those who preferred self propulsion, there were all kinds of early form of bicycle, from the penny farthing to the unsprung bone shaker, which did exactly what it says on the tin.

parts his hair with a towel

To end this list on a less serious note, this is a reference to a gentleman who is follicly challenged.

Appendix four – Solutions to Classical and other names

Here come the answers to the questions in Interlude four.

Boreas/ Aquilo, Zephyrus/Favonius, Notus/Auster, Euros/Vulturnus

These are the four main winds: north, west, south and east. And, if you insist, they come in this order: north, west, south, east. The zephyr is the west wind, a mild breeze, and the term continues to be used occasionally in modern English.

The labours of Hercules

Also known as Heracles, Hercules went mad and killed his wife Megara, and his children. As a penance, he was given twelve tasks to perform. There is a pretty comprehensive list of them in Wikipedia (search Labours of Hercules), and I select three of them for your information:

Task number one – The Nemean Lion
A huge lion was terrorising a Greek town and Hercules managed to slay it with his knife and superior strength.

Task number five – The Augean Stables
These had not been cleaned out for 30 years (don't ask), and he had to divert two rivers to accomplish the task. What happened downstream is not recorded.

Task number twelve – The Cattle of Geryon
Hercules was ordered to capture cattle belonging to the giant Geryon, which he did.

As a reward, he was given two more challenges, which was rather unkind. These accounts are based on a number of contemporary epic poems.

The island of Lesbos

This is a Greek island which in Classical mythology had Lesbos as its patron God. The poetess Sappho from Ancient times promoted relationships between women, hence the term Lesbian, based on the name of the island she lived on.

Sisyphus and Tantalus

Sisyphus was a Greek king in ancient times punished by the Gods in a rather unpleasant fashion. He was condemned to push a large rock up from Hades. When he neared the top of the incline, the stone rolled back down again, so he had to start over again and continue for all eternity.

You may be much more familiar with the name Tantalus. The modern English verb 'tantalise' goes straight back to this man, and is also related to a tantalus, which is a container for spirit bottles which can only be opened with a key, thereby 'tantalising' the thirsty who have no means of accessing it.

The mythological Tantalus was punished by the Gods by being placed in a pool with fruit tree branches hanging over it. The only problem was that every time he stretched up for the fruit they moved out of his grasp, and when he reached down for water, the level lowered so that he could not reach that either.

Nebuchadnezzar

He was a king of ancient Babylon, among whose feats was the capture of Jerusalem, which inspired the Verdi opera *Nabucco*. You may be familiar with the name as something quite different, as the term for a rather large champagne bottle, containing 1.5 litres.

Ming

Apart from being the name of a couple of Chinese takeaways, this is the name of the last great Chinese dynasty, preceded by other, including Tang, Qing and Song.

Appendix five – 'Deserted Village' answers

Answers to the words and phrases from 'The Deserted Village' coming up.

choaked with sedges – Referring to the river flowing through Auburn, 'choaked' is simply an archaic form of 'choked', in the sense of 'blocked', and sedges are grass-like plants.

sate by his fire – an old past tense form of the strong verb 'sat'. Not connected with the verb 'sate' meaning 'to fully satisfy'.

vagrant train – not the eleven-thirty at night transporting drunks back to the student halls, but a procession or succession of vagrants (those of no fixed abode) whom the village parson took in and cared for.

the spoiler's hand – the use of 'hand' here is an example of synecdoche, a mouthful of a term meaning 'using the part for the whole', so 'hand' stands for the whole person, a workman, as 'Number 10' stands for the government and 'suits' for businessmen (or lawyers, in the Netflix series). The word 'spoiler' would nowadays read as 'despoiler', someone who lays waste to or severely damages.

rood of ground – an old form of measurement. It's a unit of area equal to a quarter of an acre.

glades forlorn – a glade is an open space in a wood, a clearing. Forlorn means lost and abandoned.

humble bowers – pleasant, shaded places.

sober herd that lowed – 'sober' refers either to a gentle colour or serious, solemn. I suspect the former. and 'lowed' is the mooing noise of cattle.

the plashy spring – 'plashy' is 'splashing' and 'spring', water appearing from beneath the ground.

her wintry faggot – her winter's bundle of wood for the fire. As you will know, faggot has other meanings, but not here.

mantling bliss – 'warm, embracing happiness/contentment', refers to the inn. 'Mantling' means 'wrapped', and also refers to an ornamental piece of drapery surrounding a coat of arms.

shewed how fields were won – 'shewed' is an archaic past tense of 'show', and 'fields' are fields of battle.

furze unprofitably gay – 'furze' is a plant with spiny leaves, also known as 'gorse'. It is 'unprofitably gay' because its bright flowers serve no practical purpose. The word 'gay' simply meant cheerful or bright.

nut-brown draughts – The colour of the beer in the inn is 'nut-brown', and 'draughts' refers to the fact that it was drawn from a barrel, not taken out of a bottle.

Twelve good Rules, the game of Goose – a board game with (to me) inscrutable rules, including: 'If you land on the goose it allows you to move your piece again and again with the same number of pips until it lands on a goose-less field. You should say – 'from goose to goose I move as I choose'. However, some of the geese 'take a backward glance' so then you should 'move as you choose', but backwards. I hope that is clear.

the black gibbet – the colour is associated with the gibbet, a gallows.

distant climes – faraway places (literally climate, temperature).

wild Altama – this is probably in reference to Altamaha, a river in the state of Georgia, where there was a colony created.

that horrid shore – 'horrid' here means seriously unpleasant.

matted woods – tangled together in a tight mass, presumably hinting at impenetrable.

and kist her...babes – 'kist', not the Scottish chest for storage but an old form of 'kissed'.

boding tremblers – children who are both anxious and trembling at what might happen.

aught – anything.

cypher – read.

gauge – make physical measurements.

cot – a compressed form of 'cottage'.

slights – sleights as in magic tricks, sleights of hand.

spoiler – 'despoiler' of the land

pants – as in pants for breath, not underpants. This recalls that easily misunderstood line from Coleridge's poem 'Kubla Kahn': 'As if this earth in fast thick pants were breathing'.

labour'd mole – I should have referred to this earlier, as it forms part of the poem I quoted. It's a real teaser to end with. One of the less well-known meanings of the word, a mole is a breakwater usually made of stone, to impede the free flow of water. The phrase is pretty compressed, meaning the mole which has been laboured on by man is swiftly swept away by the forces of nature.

Other publications by Rex W Last

For up to date information, check out my website at
www.locheesoft.com. Here is a screenshot of the Home page.
Details and reviews of titles in print are on the following pages.

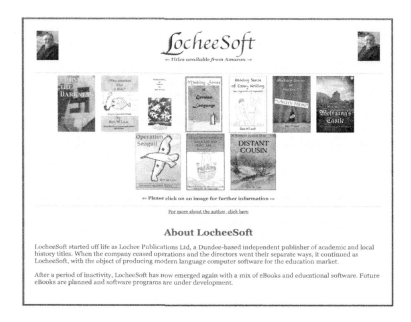

Title: *Cursing the Darkness*

Category: Fiction

Available from: www.amazon.co.uk

£1.99 (eBook)

£5.95 (paperback)

 In Nuremberg, the city which hosted the annual Nazi Party Congresses in the 1930s, a small group of like-minded individuals resolve to try and fight back against the pitiless dominance of the Nazi régime. Like many of his fellow citizens, Dr Johann Voss is tormented by his political impotence and yearns to be able to bring a group of people together to take a stand for decency and humanity. He sees a first opportunity to do so when a strange-looking patient knocks on his door in the middle of the night seeking medical attention for two bullet wounds.

The patient is Rudi, a cross-dressing cabaret comedian with a strange tale to tell, and the group expands with the recruitment of Thomas, chief mechanic of the city's transport system, who is disgusted at the cover-up of the killing of a young Jewish girl, and his friend Max, curator of the city's museum and art gallery, who has already been protecting and spiriting away significant works of art looted from Jewish homes.

Daring rescue

Together they embark on a series of daring undertakings: rescuing a Jewish family from a railway wagon in Nuremberg's marshalling yards, dramatically shaming an SS officer who had raped the family's 14-year-old daughter, and causing the spectacular public downfall of an infamous local Nazi aristocrat. Thomas is faced with the threat of death in a concentration camp and Johann is captured by the SS officer whom he shamed for his actions. The group make a courageous attempt to release Johann from the Gestapo interrogation cells.

It is now too dangerous for them to continue on their present path, but their undertakings have remarkable and unexpected consequences.

A touch of satirical humour
This potentially bleak theme is treated with sensitivity and lightness of touch, and although there are dark moments in the narrative, satirical humour plays a central role. The Nazis are caricatured even more than they are demonised, and the reader is left with a positive and life-affirming insight into the resilience of the human spirit when confronted with what appear to be impossible odds.

The title of the book draws on a quotation from Eleanor Roosevelt: 'It is better to light a single candle than to curse the darkness'.

REVIEWS

Despite the dark subject matter, the light touch, humour and compelling characters actually made for an easy read (even at bedtime!). The shortness of the chapters tempted me to read 'just one more' before retiring! Recommended.

(Harry Holbrook)

Title: *Wolfgang's Castle*

Category: Fiction

Available from: www.amazon.co.uk

£2.29 (eBook)

£5.95 (paperback)

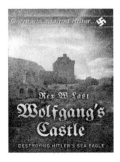

In a remote Bavarian valley in 1940, Nazi scientists are working on Project Sea Eagle to create a waterborne war machine which would spearhead a second invasion attempt of Britain. Four anti-Nazi Germans, two SOE operatives and 20 RAF officer POWs set out with severely limited resources and considerable ingenuity to destroy this 'aquaplane'.

Their target is a hybrid of sea-going craft and airplane which exploits a phenomenon called the 'ground effect', in which the vehicle is able to 'fly' a few feet above the surface at very high speeds with minimum drag.

Destroying a super weapon

The Nazis are seeking to create a high-speed landing vessel which can transport troops and materiél across the Channel in a renewed assault on the south coast of England after Hitler's decision to call off Operation Sealion, the original invasion plan.

The design and production facility for Sea Eagle is housed underground, making it inaccessible to a bombing raid - and in any event a large-scale military assault would be out of the question, given the logistics, the assumed unacceptable loss of life and the fact that British forces are at full stretch seeking to cope with a rampaging onslaught from an all-conquering Nazi Germany.

Against impossible odds

Major Archie Wellings of the SOE joins forces with two German couples and others in a bold attempt to halt Sea Eagle in its tracks, partly by turning Nazi ideology against itself, but also by a number of extremely clever ruses.

Wolfgang's Castle is the second novel in a loosely-connected series on the challenges facing Germans who were determined to undermine the Hitler régime from within. In the first, *Cursing the Darkness*, some of the characters who also appear in the second novel seek to assist those who through no fault of their own have fallen foul of the régime, and to humiliate some of the worst Nazis in positions of power and influence in the Nuremberg of the mid-1930s.

The concept of the Ground Effect Vehicle is based on experiments undertaken after the Second World War, some of which actually reached the stage of commercial production. In this novel, it is assumed that the original designs of these vehicles were worked on in Germany in secret in the 1930s and were reaching viability as military weaponry in late 1940.

Challenging issues - from the nature of patriotism to the role of women in wartime - are explored with a touch of satirical humour. It's an exciting and thought-provoking page-turner with a dash of romance.

REVIEWS

Wolfgang's Castle is a fun and exciting World War II thriller in the tradition of *Eye of the Needle*, *The Great Escape*, or *The Guns of*

Navarone. The story begins in Bavaria when a British spy plane detects suspicious activity: Hitler may be developing a revolutionary new weapon that could change the course of the war. What follows is a suspenseful series of plans, tricks, and operations to figure out what's happening in Hitler's remote research facility and to foil the dictator's objectives.

The author puts you in the scenes as the heroes impersonate Nazi officers, parachute into enemy territory, gather intelligence while hiding in snow-filled woods, and more. The story also includes just the right amount of romance.

Wolfgang's Castle is perfect for World War II buffs or anyone looking to get caught up in a gripping tale of espionage.

(Al Macy, bestselling author of *Conclusive Evidence*)

'It is part of a continuing series of novels about the endeavours of a group of Germans to counter the unstoppable advance of the Nazi régime … *Wolfgang's Castle* is a very captivating and fascinating book. I read it with rapt attention, as I was totally absorbed in it. The fast-paced storyline is amazing, and it has a lot of twists in it; this is what I love the most about this book. …

Also, this book has a good mix of action, suspense, humour, and a bit of romance in it.

I strongly recommend *Wolfgang's Castle* to all lovers of war books, and historical books. And generally, I recommend it to anyone who loves books that keep one captivated and in suspense.'

(onlinebookclub.org.)

Title: *Making Sense of Poetry Volume one*

Category: Study Skills

Available from: www.amazon.co.uk

£1.99 (eBook)

£4.95 (paperback)

This plain-speaking introduction to the study and understanding of poetry avoids academic jargon and provides a clear pathway for coming to a deeper awareness of poetry of the present and past ages. The guide is written in a clear and at times amusing style by a long-standing expert in the field. This completely revised new edition includes sidebars explaining topics discussed in greater detail, and ends with exercises and model answers.

The guide begins by examining the physical shape of a poem on the page, then moves on to a shopping list of topics:

> Vocabulary
> Imagery
> Point of view
> Personalities
> Actions
> The senses
> Position
> Rhythm and rhyme
> External references
> The unexpected

In sum, this is an invaluable introduction to the study of poetry which concentrates on acquiring practical skills.

REVIEWS

'A "must have" book which encourages the reader to explore poetry in greater depth. To pursue its meaning and thence to delight rather than bewilder.

Rex Last has written with humour and alacrity. I shall now unearth my poetry books long since assigned to dusty shelves.'

(Margaret Holman)

'I liked that the author, understanding how boring poetry could be at times, adds humour to his explanations at regular intervals. This is an effective way of teaching, as it made me appreciate what he tried to explain faster. It also made me feel refreshed while I read, as I had some good laughs. Furthermore, I liked that the author included exercises on the interpretation of poems and their solutions to enable readers to test themselves, having gained the knowledge that the book sought to teach.

There was nothing to dislike about this book, and I enjoyed it thoroughly. The author structured his message very well and executed it with perfection. ... I recommend this book for people who are interested in Poetry.'

(Reviewer, onlinebookclub.org.)

'Making Sense of Poetry is full of down-to earth wisdom. It brooks no nonsense. Its examples are perfectly chosen. The authorial voice is friendly but authoritative. The structure, with its insightful interludes, is just right. A fine educational primer.'

Robert Saxton (poet)

Title: *Making Sense of Essay Writing*

Category: Study Skills

Available from: www.amazon.co.uk

£1.99 (eBook format)

£4.95 (paperback)

The task of writing an essay falls into three stages:

> Before
>
> During and
>
> After.

Sounds obvious, but far too many students charge straight into the actual writing without planning and structuring the work required.

Before

First comes the planning process, starting with reading the title of the essay, setting out a plan, and other preparatory work.

If there is a choice of essays, it's essential (a) that you select a topic which suits you and (b) you read the question *very* carefully.

There are various types of essay which challenge the student in different ways:

> description
>
> discussion
>
> evaluation

comparison

Essays should not only be written to the length required, but they must take account of the potential reader(s).

Quotations and bibliographical material should be included where appropriate and set out in the appropriate 'house style'.

And, of course, a prerequisite for any good essay is a sound knowledge of the subject.

During

It's essential that your essay contains the following:

Introduction

Central section starting with small points building up to the main point

Conclusion.

The introduction should match the conclusion in length, and (this sounds obvious but it's so often overlooked) the conclusion has to represent a resolution of the issues posed in the introduction.

The guide offers a detailed analysis of how to use good English, style, clarity, punctuation, structure and so forth. The essay should develop in a cogent and well-organised manner and not consist of a random collection of thoughts thrown together.

After

Finally, after the essay: there is an extended section on how to check that you have done your best, breaking the process down into individual tasks.

There's also a special section on writing your essay on the

computer, essays under examination conditions, and how to write proper sentences.

Each part of the guide contains samples culled from the pages of actual student essays.

There are YouTube presentations on this subject as well as on studying poetry. Go to YouTube and in the search box, type Rex Last study skills.

Title: *Making Sense of German Language*

Category: Study Skills

Available from: www.amazon.co.uk

£3.58 (eBook)

£TBA (paperback)

This is a clear and entertaining introduction to German, aimed at anyone considering studying the language, as well as at those who are fascinated by languages and how they work.

The guide takes an innovative approach by assuming that potential readers bring a great deal of knowledge of their own to the party, starting with German words and phrases which have made their way into English (Blitzkrieg, Dachshund, Kindergarten, to name but three), and with it a fair grasp of how the Germans pronounce their words (Volkswagen, Mozart, etc).

In addition, you will be familiar with how at least one major European language - English - works, and that in itself offers valuable insights into German vocabulary, grammar and syntax.

The emphasis throughout is on explaining why German is as it is, rather than just throwing sets of 'rules' and 'exceptions' at readers and telling them that this is the way things are without teasing out the underlying structures, historical evolution, and compromises which all languages have to cope with.

No punches are pulled: German is not an easy language to master, but it all makes a deal more sense if you are aware of how and why it has evolved into its present form. The main text is dotted with 'interludes', which cover less challenging aspects of the language, like numbers and time, well-known sayings, and compound words.

The guide is rounded off with a number of parallel texts with full explanations.

There are five appendixes:

A pronunciation guide;

An extensive glossary of German words and phrases

which have made their way into English;

A glossary of technical terms for those unfamiliar with

the jargon of language learning;

A brief guide to the German spelling reform; and

Other useful resources.

Title: *She smokes like a fish*

(Second enlarged edition)

Category: Humour

Available from: www.amazon.co.uk

Price: £3.58 (eBook format)

Price £4.50 (hard copy)

 This is a compendium of mostly original material gathered over a lifetime of snapping up unconsidered trifles, including typos, headlines, odd business names, book titles, spellchecking blunders, howlers, and much more besides. In this second edition, there are new chapters and added material throughout.

All the royalties from this new edition are being donated to a very worthy cause, the Perth (Scotland) Branch of Guide Dogs.

The centrepiece of the book is a chapter 'Mr Malaprop - a man of his word' - the secretly collected mis-speakings of a former colleague, one of which forms the book's title.

She smokes like a fish places all these blunders into categories, explores the various kinds of error, warns of the perils of the computerised spellchecker and generally takes a delight in our ability to think one thing and say or write another.

Extract from the Introduction

This collection of unconsidered trifles came about when I was a Lecturer in German at Hull University many years ago.

Apart from being famous for having its own local telephone service with green and cream phone boxes and an evil-smelling glue factory which made its presence felt when the wind blew from the wrong direction, Kingston-upon-Hull boasts a daily paper with the confusing name *The Daily Mail*, because it is actually the evening paper for the locality. It has no connection to the London morning paper of the same name. I was inspired, if that's the right word, to start the collection by a small item printed in December, 1975. In those days, the Hull to York road was a well-known single-track highway with a large number of accident black spots,
and my eye caught the report of a fatal crash in which firemen had to cut the body free. The item ended with these jaw-dropping words from the original tattered cutting:

> Firemen from Market Weighton cut the body free. The dead man is believed to live in the area.

Little gems like that tend to cause a fleeting smile then vanish without trace, but I decided to try and preserve some these gems for posterity without any clear idea of what I might do with them.

To this end, I began collecting press cuttings and other material which disappeared into a cardboard box many years ago and which I have only recently unearthed. Fast forward to the new technological era of the eBook, and that offered me the opportunity to bring these fading yellowing flowers out into the harsh light of day.

Chapter headings include:

It's all in the title

Down to business

Typos

Strange but true

Lifting the Iron Curtain

Headlines

Ecclesiastical blunders

The joys of spellchecking

Mr Malaprop – a man of his word

Name that product

My anecdotage.

REVIEWS

From Amazon readers:

Absolutely fantastic, well written and incredibly funny, Enjoyed that book very much!

– o0o –

A very clever and funny book. Imaginative and in many ways innovative. Not just a list of funny sayings etc.

– o0o –

A book that has prompted many a 'laugh out loud'. I thoroughly recommend this!

– o0o –

Rex Last has shared a wealth of faux pas and verbal blunders he has collected over the years from newspapers and from overheard conversations. Together with his witty style of writing he has created a hugely enjoyable read.and prompted many a 'laugh out loud'. I eagerly await more from him.

Printed in Great Britain
by Amazon

36838254R00059